The Defective Detective

The Defective Detective

Mystery Parodies by the Great Humorists

Edited by
Steve Carper

A Citadel Press Book
Published by Carol Publishing Group

A Citadel Press Book
Published by Carol Publishing Group
Citadel Press is a registered trademark of Carol
Communications, Inc.
Editorial Offices: 600 Madison Avenue, New York, N.Y. 10022
Sales & Distribution Offices: 120 Enterprise Avenue, Secaucus,
N.J. 07094
In Canada: Canadian Manda Group, P.O. box 920, Station U,
    Toronto, Ontario M8Z 5P9
Queries regarding rights and permissions should be addressed to
Carol Publishing Group, 600 Madison Avenue, New York, N.Y. 10022

Acknowledgements and sources on page 223.

Carol Publishing Group books are available at special discounts
for bulk purchases, for sales promotions, fund raising, or
educational purposes. Special editions can be created to specifications.
For details, contact: Special Sales Department, Carol Publishing
Group, 120 Enterprise Avenue, Secaucus, N.J. 07094

Manufactured in the United States of America
10 9 8 7 6 5 4 3 2 1

Library of Congress Cataloging-in-Publication Data

The Defective detective : mystery parodies by the great humorists /
    edited by Steve Carper.
        p. cm.
    ISBN 0-8065-1367-5
        1. Detective and mystery stories, American.   2. Detective and
mystery stories, English.   3. Humorous stories, American.
4. Humorous stories, English.   5. Parodies.   I. Carper, Steve.
PS648.D4D44 1992
813'.087208—dc20   92-17734
                                                            CIP

Contents

INTRODUCTION   9
WOODY ALLEN
    "Match Wits with Inspector Ford"   15
COREY FORD
    "The Third Door from the Left'   23
S.J. PERELMAN
    "Farewell, My Lovely Appetizer"   31
ALAN COREN
    "Doctor No Will See You Now"   41
OGDEN NASH
    "Don't Guess, Let Me Tell You"   49
IRA WALLACH
    "Me, the Judge"   53
STEPHEN LEACOCK
    "Maddened By Mystery: or, The Defective
    Detective"   61

HENRY BEARD
  "The Big Recall"   73
CHRISTOPHER WARD
  "The Pink Murder Case"   97
JAMES THURBER
  "The White Rabbit Caper"   105
GARRISON KEILLOR
  "Jack Schmidt, Arts Administrator"   117
BRET HARTE
  "The Stolen Cigar Case"   129
JOHN HARRIS
  "Monastic Mayhem: An Echo of Eco"   141
JON L. BREEN
  "Breakneck"   151
ROBERT BENCHLEY
  "The Mystery of the Poisoned Kipper"   157
JIM DAVIS AND RON TUTHILL
  "Babes and Bullets"   163
BOB AND RAY
  "Mr. Treet, Chaser of Lost People"   177
JOHN SLADEK
  "The Purloined Butter"   185
E.C. BENTLEY
  "Greedy Night"   189
FRAN LEBOWITZ
  "In Hot Pursuit"   205
P.G. WODEHOUSE
  "About These Mystery Stories"   213

The Defective Detective

Introduction

BY STEVE CARPER

QUICK. Think of a private eye, a cop, a spy, an amateur sleuth. What images come to mind? They're more than likely not to be from a specific figure but from an amalgam of hundreds of generic examples, a combination of characters from a lifetime of reading books, watching movies and vegging out in front of the TV set. Congratulations. You've just created your own parody.

Parodying mysteries is so easy that many mystery writers do it to themselves inadvertently: the trick is to make it biting and funny. For that we need to turn to humorists. Humorists, fortunately, have always been happy to oblige. I have on my shelves copies of every major collection of parodies published in the 20th century. Mysteries are a target in virtually every one.

9

Why the mystery? Simple. Parody depends upon instant recognitions of literary tics, traits, foibles and affectations. Mysteries thrive under this democracy of the spirit while literature tends to have a surprisingly short shelf life. Parodies of mysteries live on; not so the ones based on all too serious works.

The single most famous book of parodies ever written— Max Beerbohm's 1912 *A Christmas Garland*—contains spoofs of Maurice Hewlett and A. C. Benson, Edmund Gosse and Arnold Bennett, names today known almost solely because Beerbohm thought enough of them to mock. Beerbohm should have chosen his targets with an eye to posterity. By 1912 Sherlock Holmes had already been for a quarter century the most famous literary figure in the world.

While high literature may sit dustily on library shelves, the mystery never goes out of style. For all intents and purposes the modern mystery begins with Holmes, and the later-to-be-Sir Arthur Conan Doyle's now more than 100-year-old creation is as famous today as he was in the late Victorian era, when crowds would line up outside book stalls, waiting for the new issue of *Strand* magazine to go on sale.

The genius of Holmes is that he is a collection of symbols. Everything about him is a picture. The deer-stalker hat. The cape. The pipe. The violin. The needle. The patriotic V.R. done in bullet marks upon the wall. Dr. Watson. Mrs. Hudson. The Baker Street Irregulars. The everlasting Victorian, fog-strewn playground of hansom cabs and moonlit moors. No matter that some of these are the invention of later illustrators and playwrights. They were real enough to the Victorians themselves, and the surfeit of Sherlocks given to us over the years in the movies and television has locked these symbols into our synapses. What Doyle did was give the mystery a common language, an identity, that made it instantly recognizable as a genre all its own.

And with Holmes also begins the mystery parody. Only a half dozen or so Holmes stories had appeared by May 1892, when Robert Barr published "Detective Stories Gone Wrong: The Adventures of Sherlaw Kombs." Sherlaw Kombs. Well, it was a simpler age. Even if the name wasn't an immediate giveaway, the character would be. The violin playing, the contempt for Scotland Yard, the miraculous deductions concerning the occupation of the visitor, all are purely Holmesian. And, setting the pattern for all future Holmesian parodies, the brilliant solution to the case is widely inaccurate.

For some reason writers with a darkly cynical view of the human condition have been drawn to satirizing Sherlock in the century since. Mark Twain, O. Henry, Kingsley Amis, John Lennon, and William Kotzwinkle have done so, in addition to those included in this volume. Holmes' perfection seems to act as a goad for them much as the platitudes of politicians serve to drive the daily needs of editorial cartoonists. The balance is exquisite. We evidently require the parody as much as we do the original.

From Holmes the mystery genre burgeoned. By the 1920s readers were already sick of mystery conventions: the secret passages, oriental villains, trick timetables, and murderous butlers that later feeble imitators of Doyle foisted on the public. The '20s were also the heyday of the humor magazine, providing a vast continuous market to the new class of professional wits, such as the denizens of the Algonquin Round Table. The two forces collided, a storm front producing an awareness that the generic mystery was as much fun to spoof as the larger-than-life eccentricities of Holmes himself. Writers such as Robert Benchley, Corey Ford, Stephen Leacock and P. G. Wodehouse spoofed the '20s detectives, creating situations almost as ridiculous as the mystery writers themselves did, but with deliberate humor.

Simultaneously, the 1920s saw a reaction to the standard silliness of British country house mysteries from inside the mystery community. From the pages of *Black Mask* magazine stepped a new breed of detective who came to be known as private eyes, a crude, brash, vulgar figure created by crude, brash, and vulgar writers: Carroll John Daly, Raoul Whitfield, Frederick Nebel, and most famously, Dashiell Hammett. In Raymond Chandler's immortal line, "Hammett took murder out of the Venetian vase and dropped it into the alley."

The private eye calls to mind almost as many cliché images as does Holmes. The cheap office with the bottle of rye in the bottom desk drawer. The sultry babe with the endless gams and a figure that defies all the laws of mathematics, not to mention gravity. The corrupt cop, smashing his knuckles into the eye's mouth. The fedora. The .45. The rain-washed streets of nighttime L.A. All told in a hyperbolic prose compounded of wisecracks, made-up slang, and non-stop metaphors.

The melodic vernacular of the private eye proved an irresistible lure for parodists. Parodists must love the English language, must have an ear as finely tuned for the rhythms and nuances of other writers' prose as painters must have for the colors and textures of surrounding landscapes.

The high voltage reign of the private eye coincided with the rise of that most hyperbolic of humorists, S. J. Perelman. Perelman specialized in reproducing the strange contortions by which pulp writers, advertising execs, and scenario artists tormented the purity of the English language. His private eye parodies set the tone for all to follow.

Follow they have, with every conceivable degree of sophistication, from Henry Beard in the pages of the

National Lampoon to Woody Allen in the pages of *The New Yorker* to the regular cast of idiots in the pages of *Mad* magazine. If Holmes is our great import from England, then the tough guy image is America's most famous export to the rest of the world. I leave to you to decide who got the best of that bargain. But if brashness symbolizes the best of America, then I submit the parody is part of that national heritage.

Holmes, whodunits, and private eyes remain the heart of the mystery and therefore of the mystery parody; this volume is heavily weighted toward them. But the genre knows no bounds, expanding to take in whatever darknesses are lurking in the national psyche.

Since the 1920s floods of psychological suspense chillers, police procedurals, spies both hot and cold, and recently technothrillers have washed across the chain bookstores in the malls, our equivalent of the Victorians' book stalls. Spies and cops and others are included herein. I'm not sure what's delaying the technothriller parody, but I'm sure it's on the way. It must be. Mysteries are part of the common currency of our culture. In America we celebrate what we love by making fun of it. Here then is a celebration of the mystery.

The parodies you're about to read span the century from 1902 to 1986; come from both sides of the Atlantic Ocean; parody individual authors like Mickey Spillane and Dick Francis, noted characters like Philo Vance and James Bond, and entire subgenres; appear in the form of stories, scripts, and poems; and generally resemble one another not in the least little bit save for one critical detail: I found them all to be funny. Part of the fun of putting the anthology together was balancing as many styles of and approaches to humor as I could cram in.

This collection exists because I've been waiting all my life for somebody else to do it and nobody ever did.

Enjoy.

Woody Allen

Match Wits with Inspector Ford

At one point in the 1970s Woody Allen became so popular that he was given the ultimate American accolade—he was turned into a comic strip. Everybody's favorite ineffectual intellectual, Woody Allen one-upped Stephen Leacock and Robert Benchley by extending their mutual pose of bumbling schnook to nightclub routines, the Broadway stage and full-length movies. Especially the movies. After *Take the Money and Run, Play It Again, Sam, Bananas,* and *Sleeper,* he was hailed as the funniest comedian to come along since the heyday of the Marx Brothers. America adopted him as it would a lost and sad-eyed puppy. Woody joined the ranks of those known with only a single name, like Dylan or Picasso.

Somewhere between the early Woody Allen, nightclub comic, and today's Woody Allen, austere auteur, came Woody Allen, writer of humorous gems. Like Perelman

before him, he found a home in *The New Yorker* and a few
selected alternate magazines and favored us with a series of
short, highly literate, and intensely funny pieces. Three
collections of Woodyisms exist (*Getting Even, Without Feathers,* and *Side Effects*) and parodies abound in them.

To certain readers (you know who you are), the only true
mysteries are those that are intellectual games, like
crossword puzzles with characters. As even those sometimes prove to be insufficiently mechanical, many authors
have turned out entire books of short puzzles, in which the
only point is spotting the one clue that leads to the identity
of the murderer. Attacking intellectual pointlessness is
Woody Allen's stock-in-trade, so be prepared to unbend
your brains as you "Match Wits with Inspector Ford."

* * *

The Case of the Murdered Socialite

INSPECTOR FORD burst into the study. On the floor was the
body of Clifford Wheel, who apparently had been struck
from behind with a croquet mallet. The position of the
body indicated that the victim had been surprised in the
act of singing "Sorrento" to his goldfish. Evidence showed
there had been a terrible struggle that had twice been
interrupted by phone calls, one a wrong number and one
asking if the victim was interested in dance lessons.

Before Wheel had died, he had dipped his finger into
the inkwell and scrawled out a message: "Fall Sale Prices
Drastically Reduced—Everything Must Go!"

"A businessman to the end," mused Ives, his man-
servant, whose elevator shoes, curiously enough, made him
two inches shorter.

The door to the terrace was open and footprints led
from there, down the hall and into a drawer.

"Where were you when it happened, Ives?"

"In the kitchen. Doing the dishes." Ives produced some suds from his wallet to corroborate his story.

"Did you hear anything?"

"He was in there with some men. They were arguing over who was the tallest. I thought I heard Mr. Wheel start yodeling and Mosley, his business partner, began yelling, 'My God, I'm going bald!' Next thing I knew, there was a harp glissando and Mr. Wheel's head came rolling out onto the lawn. I heard Mr. Mosley threaten him. He said if Mr. Wheel touched his grapefruit again, he would not cosign a bank loan for him. I think he killed him."

"Does the terrace door open from the inside or from the outside?" Inspector Ford asked Ives.

"From the outside. Why?"

"Exactly as I suspected. I now realized it was you, not Mosley, who killed Clifford Wheel."

How Did Inspector Ford Know?

Because of the layout of the house, Ives could not have sneaked up behind his employer. He would have had to sneak up in front of him, at which time Mr. Wheel would have stopped singing "Sorrento" and used the mallet on Ives, a ritual they had gone through many times.

A Curious Riddle

Apparently, Walker was a suicide. Overdose of sleeping pills. Still, something seemed amiss to Inspector Ford. Perhaps it was the position of the body. Inside the TV set, looking out. On the floor was a cryptic suicide note. "Dear Edna, My woolen suit itches me, and so I have decided to take my own life. See that our son finishes all his push-ups. I leave you my entire fortune, with the exception of my porkpie hat, which I hereby donate to the planetarium. Please don't feel sorry for me, as I enjoy being dead and much prefer it to paying rent. Goodbye, Henry. P.S. This may not be the time to bring it up, but I have every reason to believe that your brother is dating a Cornish hen."

Edna Walker bit her lower lip nervously. "What do you make of it, Inspector?"

Inspector Ford looked at the bottle of sleeping pills on the night table. "How long had your husband been an insomniac?"

"For years. It was psychological. He was afraid that if he closed his eyes, the city would paint a white line down him."

"I see. Did he have any enemies?"

"Not really. Except for some gypsies who ran a tearoom on the outskirts of town. He insulted them once by putting on a pair of earmuffs and hopping up and down in place on their sabbath."

Inspector Ford noticed a half-finished glass of milk on the desk. It was still warm. "Mrs. Walker, is your son away at college?"

"I'm afraid not. He was expelled last week for immoral conduct. It came as quite a surprise. They caught him trying to immerse a dwarf in tartar sauce. That's one thing they won't tolerate at an Ivy League school."

"And one thing I won't tolerate is murder. Your son is under arrest."

Why Did Inspector Ford Suspect
Walker's Son Had Killed Him?

Mr. Walker's body was found with cash in his pockets. A man who was going to commit suicide would be sure to take a credit card and sign for everything.

The Stolen Gem

The glass case was shattered and the Bellini Sapphire was missing. The only clues left behind at the museum were a blond hair and a dozen fingerprints, all pinkies. The guard explained that he had been standing there when a black-clad figure crept up behind him and struck him over the head with some notes for a speech. Just before losing consciousness, he thought he had heard a man's voice say, "Jerry, call your mother," but he could not be sure. Apparently, the thief had entered through the skylight and walked down the wall with suction shoes, like a human fly. The museum guards always kept an enormous fly swatter for just such occasions, but this time they had been fooled.

"Why would anyone want the Bellini Sapphire?" the museum curator asked. "Don't they know it's cursed?"

"What's this about a curse?" Inspector Ford was quick to ask.

"The sapphire was originally owned by a sultan who died under mysterious circumstances when a hand reached out of a bowl of soup he was eating and strangled him. The next owner was an English lord who was found one day by his wife growing upside down in a window box. Nothing was heard of the stone for a while; then it turned up years later in the possession of a Texas millionaire, who was brushing his teeth when he suddenly caught fire. We purchased the sapphire only last month, but the curse seemed to be working still, because shortly after we obtained it, the entire board of trustees at the museum formed a conga line and danced off a cliff."

"Well," Inspector Ford said, "it may be an unlucky jewel, but it's valuable, and if you want it back, go to Handleman's Delicatessen and arrest Leonard Handleman. You'll find that the sapphire is in his pocket."

How Did Inspector Ford Know
Who the Jewel Thief Was?

The previous day, Leonard Handleman had remarked, "Boy, if I had a large sapphire, I could get out of the delicatessen business."

The Macabre Accident

"I just shot my husband," wept Cynthia Freem as she stood over the body of the burly man in the snow.

"How did it happen?" asked Inspector Ford, getting right to the point.

"We were hunting. Quincy loved to hunt, as did I. We got separated momentarily. The bushes were overgrown. I guess I thought he was a woodchuck. I blasted away. It was too late. As I was removing his pelt, I realized we were married."

"Hmm," mused Inspector Ford, glancing at the footprints in the snow. "You must be a very good shot. You managed to plug him right between the eyebrows."

"Oh, no, it was lucky. I'm really quite an amateur at that sort of thing."

"I see." Inspector Ford examined the dead man's possessions. In his pocket there was some string, also an apple from 1904 and instructions on what to do if you wake up next to an Armenian.

"Mrs. Freem, was this your husband's first hunting accident?"

"His first fatal one, yes. Although once in the Canadian Rockies, an eagle carried off his birth certificate."

"Did your husband wear a toupee?"

"Not really. He would usually carry it with him and produce it if challenged in an argument. Why?"

"He sounds eccentric."

"He was."

"Is that why you killed him?"

*How Did Inspector Ford Know
It Was No Accident?*

An experienced hunter like Quincy Freem would never have stalked deer in his underwear. Actually, Mrs. Freem had bludgeoned him to death at home while he was playing the spoons and had tried to make it look like a hunting accident by dragging his body to the words and leaving a copy of *Field & Stream* nearby. In her haste, she had forgotten to dress him. Why he had been playing the spoons in his underwear remains a mystery.

The Bizarre Kidnapping

Half-starved, Kermit Kroll staggered into the living room of his parents' home, where they waited anxiously with Inspector Ford.

"Thanks for paying the ransom, folks," Kermit said. "I never thought I'd get out of there alive."

"Tell me about it," the inspector said.

"I was on my way downtown to have my hat blocked when a sedan pulled up and two men asked me if I wanted to see a horse that could recite the Gettysburg Address. I said sure and got in. Next thing, I'm chloroformed and wake up somewhere tied to a chair and blindfolded."

Inspector Ford examined the ransom note. "Dear Mom and Dad, Leave $50,000 in a bag under the bridge on Decatur Street. If there is no bridge on Decatur Street, please build one. I am being treated well, given shelter and good food, although last night the clams casino were overcooked. Send the money quickly, because if they don't hear from you within several days, the man who now makes up my bed will strangle me. Yours, Kermit. P.S. This is no joke. I am enclosing a joke so you will be able to tell the difference."

"Do you have any idea at all as to where you were being held?"

"No, I just kept hearing an odd noise outside the window."

"Odd?"

"Yes. You know the sound a herring makes when you lie to it?"

"Hmm," reflected Inspector Ford. "And how did you finally escape?"

"I told them I wanted to go to the football game but I only had a single ticket. They said okay, as long as I kept the blindfold on and promised to return by midnight. I complied, but during the third quarter, the Bears had a big lead, so I left and made my way back here."

"Very interesting," Inspector Ford said. "Now I know this kidnapping was a put-up job. I believe you're in on it and are splitting the money."

How Did Inspector Ford Know?

Although Kermit Kroll did still live with his parents, they were eighty and he was sixty. Actual kidnappers would never abduct a sixty-year-old child, as it makes no sense.

Woody Allen. *Without Feathers.* NY: Warner Books, 1976.

Corey Ford

The Third Door from the Left

Like so many of the humorists of the 1920s, Corey Ford launched his career on the staff of a college humor magazine, the *Jester* at Columbia University, an institution from which he escaped without the customary diploma. The lack didn't constrain his career, which eventually numbered some thirty books, including several serious studies of the spy trade.

Parodies were Ford's specialty, starting from his first book at the tender age of twenty-three, *Three Rousing Cheers for the Rollo Boys,* lampooning the then wildly popular Rover Boys adventures. He set his sights higher when he started working for *Vanity Fair* magazine, where he eventually busied himself at the rate of two articles a month. One of the two was always a biting parody of some of the day's best sellers, including Hemingway, Dreiser, and Mencken. A new byline was necessary for these:

My method of choosing a pseudonym was to shut my eyes, open the New York Telephone Directory at random, and put my finger on a name. The name turned out to be Runkleschemlz, so I threw the phone book away and thought up "John Riddell," a clever rearrangement of the letters of my own name.

Three John Riddell collections can be found: *Meaning No Offense, In the Worst Possible Taste* (a title taken from a review!), and *The John Riddell Murder Case*, which featured a parody of S. S. Van Dine's Philo Vance mysteries wrapped as a framing tale around the reprinted parodies.

Ford eventually let his Riddell persona take over the parody business, preferring to send forth a stream of high quality nonsense under his own name. Early on, however, before his personality split, the nonsense and the parody emerged wrapped inextricably around each other. Convoluted mysteries were the vogue in the mid-1920s, with sinister Orientals, mistaken identities, secret passages, and a host of other clichés, hoary even then, the norm. (See P. G. Wodehouse's *About These Mystery Stories* for more on '20s stereotypes.) Ford takes these clichés to almost surreal heights in this dizzying compilation of confusion.

* * *

A THRILLING DETECTIVE SERIAL
WHEREIN THE FATES OF A MAN
AND A WOMAN ARE JUGGLED
IN THE TANGLED WEB OF A
MURDER MYSTERY, AND
DEATH TAKES HIS GRIM
TOLL

By the Author of "The Man with the Longitudinal Scar,"

*"Tombstones that Lie," and "100 Helpful
Hints for Expectant Mothers."*

Characters in the Story Thus Far:

RALPH FAIRFAX, a keen-witted cub reporter who is infatuated with

FAITH ARDSLEIGH, the beautiful but unspoiled daughter of
Dr. Eliot. Evelyn believes firmly in the innocence of

MRS. HUMPHREY, the uncle of Faith and a wealthy society
worker who was found murdered in the palatial library
of his home at 1318 Grand Concourse, Fordham, not far
from the cottage of

EDGAR ALLAN POE, a writer, with a small blunt instrument
like a pencil sharpener.

"LIGHT-FINGERED" LAURA, faithful old servant in the
home of John Fayerweather and head of a band of
smugglers, confesses to the District Attorney, Mrs.
Humphrey, that on the eve of his death

"CHICK" O'MALLEY, the driver of the taxi-cab, is none
other than

FAITH ARDSLEIGH, the brother of Ralph, a mysterious
Spanish woman who disappeared shortly after the robbery. Dr. Eliot snitches. Cross-examination of "Light-
Fingered" Laura, his mother, discloses that the District
Attorney swallowed certain "White Powders," resulting
in the Wall Street explosion. Mr. Faucet denies everything. Now go on with the story:

FOR A MOMENT neither man spoke. The sputtering candle
on the teakwood table had burned low, and in the dim
reflection their white, set faces were motionless. The older
man grasped a pearl-handled revolver in his long, thin
fingers, but no muscles stirred in the expressionless face of
his opponent across the table. The hand of the younger of

the pair was closed upon a revolver with a pearl handle, but the man opposite him did not flinch. Tense, poised, crouched like a cat about to spring, each waited for the other to make a move.

A low moaning swept the lofty, heavy-carpeted library; a distant shutter banged in the equinoxial storm, and from the dim recesses of the cellar came the sound of someone chopping wood. The musty halls were filled with memories for young Revelstoke...memories of a long and bitter line of Revelstokes, memories of Tragedy and Sorrow and Hate. Sir Renfrew Revelstoke, his grandfather, had hung himself here in the chimney corner; his thin dry body still swung from a rusty nail and rattled in the wind. His Great-Aunt Pamela, poisoned thirty-three years come Michaelmas, was lying sprawled in a unique posture over the sectional bookcase. From the waste-basket projected the legs of his ne'er-do-well brother who had slit his wrists after strangling his sister and cramming her body up this very fireplace; the draft had not worked well since. These memories were fragrant still, as the two men faced each other silently across the teakwood table. A quaint Oriental dagger dropped from the ceiling and quivered upright between them. Neither man stirred.

The clock struck thirteen times, and a blinding flash of lightning revealed a dim figure silhouetted in the long French windows. Furtively he glanced about him, and slowly drew shut the windows again, letting the latch slide into place as silently as a cat. He placed a black cigar between his teeth; in the sudden flare of the match his face was revealed for only an instant, but in that fraction of time he had lit his cigar.

"Has Dr. Cruikshank returned yet?" asked Inspector Boyd.

"No," replied Dr. Cruikshank, "but I think I have a clue."

"Was it an inside job?" asked Inspector Boyd, rolling the cigar around his mouth.

"I have examined the body," replied the elderly physician, "and I cannot find any mark of violence, except, possibly that the head is missing."

"Then we must find the head," snapped the Inspector, lighting his cigar. "Who was murdered?"

"I think it was Inspector Boyd," replied Dr. Cruikshank after a moment's hesitation.

"Murdered!" uttered Inspector Boyd. "Oh, my God!"

"Will that be all, sir?" asked Dr. Cruikshank.

"That will be all," replied Dr. Cruikshank, bowing himself out.

From a trap-door under the table a file of Chinese ran out and disappeared through the door of the grandfather's clock. Quick as a cat the Inspector snatched a pocket-mirror, flung himself into a deep arm-chair with his back to the door, and, slyly adjusting his mirror so that the entire room was visible behind him, he whipped out his revolver and fired three times, followed by a ripple of polite conversation and modulated laughter. The ballroom door was flung open and the Countess Marya rushed in, grasping her white throat in her bare hands and clutching the air before her. "My pearls—" she gasped, and fainted.

"Come in," replied Inspector Boyd, lighting his cigar.

Across the teakwood table the two men faced each other, tense, waiting, each striving to read behind his opponent's eyes the secret plan that was in his mind. Every fiber was keyed to the highest pitch, every muscle expectant and ready, like a coiled spring. Across the lawn galloped a huge police-dog, smeared with phosphorus and baying like a hound of hell.

"Just as I thought," said Inspector Boyd, firing his revolver. "The murderer of Henry Twillerby is still alive. *He is in that closet now!*"

From above them came a sound of scuffling and clanking of chains, then a groan and the thud of a heavy body falling. Slowly a section of the book-case opened out, and from the shadows a gloved hand reached for the light switch. Instantly the room was plunged in darkness.

"Is Inspector Boyd here?" cried the medium in a slow, quavering, moaning treble, "I want Inspector Boyd—"

"Gad!" mutterred the Inspector, mopping his brow, "Gad! how did she learn that?"

"I am the spirit of Henry Twillerby," continued the medium in a blood-curdling shriek, as three shots rang out and the Inspector groped for the light switch. The flood of illumination revealed an empty room.

"You may as well confess," snarled Inspector Boyd. "We've got the goods on you! Ever see *this* before?" holding up an armbone. "Where's the rest of the body? Out with it, man!"

"And if I refuse?" parried Dr. Cruikshank, and fired. The Inspector measured his length on the floor.

"I'll admit you were pretty clever," sneered the Inspector, "but I was just a *little* bit cleverer. Two can play at that game," he hissed, snapping the irons on the prostrate form of Dr. Cruikshank, as the door opened and Dr. Cruikshank entered as breathless as a cat, the blood streaming from a cut over his left temple.

"Stick up your mitts and not a word out of your trap," he commanded in a whisper, "or I'll pull the trigger and empty the contents of this whole magazine (*adv.*)."

"That is not a gun in your pocket," sneered the Inspector, "that is only a corkscrew. Never in my checkered career have I been so completely hood-winked."

"You sure are a cool one," admitted Dr. Cruikshank. "It appears this man I am tracking is nobody's fool."

The bland Oriental mask of the man before him gave forth no sign of his emotions.

"Well, where did you get it?" persisted the detective, removing a vicious hand-made dagger from the Chinaman's trouser-leg. "Come clean, now."

Mr. Chang thought a moment. "Ah, that would be telling," he parried, rolling a wheatstraw paper cigarette with characteristic calm, and fired. Dr. Cruikshank clutched his stomach.

"Don't mind me," he muttered thickly. "I'm all right, don't mind me. Get that man. Don't mind me, I'm all right... I'm all..." but a gush of blood choked the dying words in his throat.

"I perceive I have been cleverly planted," grinned Inspector Boyd, as his daughter descended the staircase in negligee and stared at the body.

"Father!" she screamed, biting off the end of a cigar, and fired.

Dr. Cruikshank toyed with the smoking revolver and coolly contemplated the body before him. "An ugly business, Inspector," he remarked solemnly. "A very ugly business. Certainly our luck has not changed for the better."

"My God, who are you?" gasped Inspector Boyd.

"I am your daughter," replied Dr. Cruikshank simply.

Silent, tense, white-lipped, the two opponents faced each other across the teakwood table. Inspector Boyd held his cigar suddenly at arm's length, eyed it suspiciously, sniffed the air again, and then glared at the motionless figures. The candle sputtered and went out.

"We must get rid of those two men, Doctor," he said calmly. "They've been dead for over a week."

(Who is Wu Chu Fang? What were the contents of that will? How is your uncle? A new and fascinating "Inspector Boyd" story will be published in an early issue over our dead body. Order your copy NOW!)

Corey Ford. *The Gazelle's Ears.* NY: George H. Doran Co., 1926.

S. J. Perelman

Farewell, My Lovely Appetizer

Perelman the humorist, Perelman the Marx Brothers co-hort, Perelman the Academy Award-winning screenwriter. Sidney Joseph Perelman may have swapped hats, but his literate, assailing, convoluted style remained idiosyncratically distinctive—and funny. At his best, Perelman was, simply, the best: the funniest humorist of the 20th century.

Perelman's early work is filled with parody. He loved the extremes to which playwrights and journalists, ad men and pedants could push his beloved English language. The white heat of the parodies suited his own hyperbolic style as well. Even on his favorite subject—himself—Perelman resorted to parody, here of the backwards, adjective-strewn style that *Time* magazine once affected:

> Button-cute, rapier-keen, wafer-thin, and pauper-poor is S. J. Perelman, whose tall, stooping figure is

better known to the twilit half-world of five continents than to Publishers' Row. That he possesses the power to become invisible to finance companies; that his laboratory is tooled up to manufacture Frankenstein-type monsters on an incredible scale; and that he owns one of the rare mouths in which butter has never melted are legends treasured by every schoolboy.

Like many humorists, Perelman was fascinated by the whiz-bang prose, wisecracks, slang, and unreality of the world of the hardboiled private eyes who proliferated in the 1940s. He appropriated the title of one of Raymond Chandler's best books, *Farewell, My Lovely*, took the trimmings off of Dashiell Hammett's *The Maltese Falcon*, added the clichés of any number of lesser writers, and wedded them to his own obsessions with the inanities of advertising prose for this inimitable piece of Perelmania.

* * *

ADD SMORGASBITS to your ought-to-know department, the newest of the three Betty Lee products. What in the world! Just small mouthsize pieces of herring and of pinkish tones. We crossed our heart and promised not to tell the secret of their tinting.— *Clementine Paddleford's food column in the* Herald Tribune.

The "Hush-Hush" Blouse. We're very hush-hush about his name, but the celebrated shirtmaker who did it for us is famous on two continents for blouses with details like those deep yoke folds, the wonderful shoulder pads, the shirtband bowl!—Russeks adv. in the *Times*.

I CAME DOWN the sixth-floor corridor of the Arbogast Building, past the World Wide Noodle Corporation,

Zwinger & Rumsey, Accountants, and the Ace Secretarial Service, Mimeographing Our Specialty. The legend on the ground-glass panel next door said, "Atlas Detective Agency, Noonan & Driscoll," but Snapper Driscoll had retired two years before with a .38 slug between the shoulders, donated by a snowbird in Tacoma, and I owned what good will the firm had. I let myself into the crummy anteroom we kept to impress clients, growled good morning at Birdie Claflin.

"Well, you certainly look like something the cat dragged in," she said. She had a quick tongue. She also had eyes like dusty lapis lazuli, taffy hair, and a figure that did things to me. I kicked open the bottom drawer of her desk, let two inches of rye trickle down my craw, kissed Birdie square on her lush, red mouth, and set fire to a cigarette.

"I could go for you, sugar," I said slowly. Her face was veiled, watchful. I stared at her ears, liking the way they were joined to her head. There was something complete about them; you knew they were there for keeps. When you're a private eye, you want things to stay put.

"Any customers?"

"A woman by the name of Sigrid Bjornsterne said she'd be back. A looker."

"Swede?"

"She'd like you to think so."

I nodded toward the inner office to indicate that I was going in there, and went in there. I lay down on the davenport, took off my shoes, and bought myself a shot from the bottle I kept underneath. Four minutes later, an ash-blonde with eyes the color of unset opals, in a Nettie Rosenstein basic black dress and a baum-marten stole, burst in. Her bosom was heaving and it looked even better that way. With a gasp she circled the desk, hunting for some place to hide, and then, spotting the wardrobe where I keep a change of bourbon, ran into it. I got up and wandered out into the anteroom. Birdie was deep in a crossword puzzle.

"See anyone come in here?"

"Nope." There was a thoughtful line between her brows. "Say, what's a five-letter word meaning 'trouble'?"

"Swede," I told her, and went back inside. I waited the length of time it would take a small, not very bright, boy to recite *Ozymandias,* and, inching carefully along the wall, took a quick gander out of the window. A thin galoot with stooping shoulders was being very busy reading a paper outside the Gristede store two blocks away. He hadn't been there an hour ago, but then, of course, neither had I. He wore a size seven dove-colored hat from Browning King, a tan Wilson Brothers shirt with pale-blue stripes, a J. Press foulard with a mixed red-and-white figure, dark-blue Interwoven socks, and an unshined pair of ox-blood London Character shoes. I let a cigarette burn down between my fingers until it made a small red mark, and then I opened the wardrobe.

"Hi," the blonde said lazily. "You Mike Noonan?" I made a noise that could have been "Yes," and waited. She yawned. I thought things over, decided to play it safe. I yawned. She yawned back, then, settling into a corner of the wardrobe, went to sleep. I let another cigarette burn down until it made a second red mark beside the first one, and then I woke her up. She sank into a chair, crossing a pair of gams that tightened my throat as I peered under the desk at them.

"Mr. Noonan," she said, "you—you've got to help me."

"My few friends call me Mike," I said pleasantly.

"Mike." She rolled the syllable on her tongue. "I don't believe I've ever heard that name before. Irish?"

"Enough to know the difference between a gossoon and a bassoon."

"What *is* the difference?" she asked. I dummied up; I figured I wasn't giving anything away for free. Her eyes narrowed. I shifted my two hundred pounds slightly, lazily set fire to a finger, and watched it burn down. I could see she was admiring the interplay of muscles in my shoulders. There wasn't any extra fat on Mike Noonan, but I wasn't telling *her* that. I was playing it safe until I knew where we stood. When she spoke again, it came with a rush. "Mr. Noonan, he thinks I'm trying to poison him. But I swear the herring was pink—I took it out of the jar myself. If I could only find out how they tinted it. I offered them money, but they wouldn't tell."

"Suppose you take it from the beginning," I suggested. She drew a deep breath. "You've heard of the golden spintria of Hadrian?" I shook my head. "It's a tremendously valuable coin believed to have been given by the Emperor Hadrian to one of his proconsuls, Caius Vitellius. It disappeared about 150 A.D., and eventually passed into the possession of Hucbald the Fat. After the sack of Adrianople by the Turks, it was loaned by a man named Shapiro to the court physician, or hakim, of Abdul Mahmoud. Then it dropped out of sight for nearly five hundred years, until last August, when a dealer in secondhand books named Lloyd Thursday sold it to my husband."

"And now it's gone again," I finished.

"No," she said. "At least, it was lying on the dresser when I left, an hour ago." I leaned back, pretending to fumble a carbon out of the desk, and studied her legs again. This was going to be a lot more intricate than I had thought. Her voice got huskier. "Last night I brought home a jar of Smorgasbits for Walter's dinner. You know them?"

"Small mouth-size pieces of herring and of pinkish tones, aren't they?"

Her eyes darkened, lightened, got darker again. "How did you know?"

"I haven't been a private op nine years for nothing, sister. Go on."

"I—I knew right away something was wrong when

Walter screamed and upset his plate. I tried to tell him the
herring was supposed to be pink, but he carried on like a
madman. He's been suspicious of me since—well, ever
since I made him take out that life insurance."

"What was the face amount of the policy?"

"A hundred thousand. But it carried a triple-indemnity
clause in case he died by sea food. Mr. Noonan—Mike—"
her tone caressed me—"I've got to win back his confidence. You could find out how they tinted that herring."

"What's in it for me?"

"Anything you want." The words were a whisper. I
leaned over, poked open her handbag, counted off five
grand.

"This'll hold me for a while," I said. "If I need any more,
I'll beat my spoon on the high chair." She got up. "Oh,
while I think of it, how does this golden spintria of yours tie
in with the herring?"

"It doesn't," she said calmly. "I just threw it in for
glamour." She trailed past me in a cloud of scent that
retailed at ninety rugs the ounce. I caught her wrist, pulled
her up to me.

"I go for girls named Sigrid with opal eyes," I said.

"Where'd you learn my name?"

"I haven't been a private snoop twelve years for nothing,
sister."

"It was nine last time."

"It seemed like twelve till you came along." I held the
clinch until a faint wisp of smoke curled out of her ears,
pushed her through the door. Then I slipped a pint of rye
into my stomach and a heater into my kick and went
looking for a bookdealer named Lloyd Thursday. I knew
he had no connection with the herring caper, but in my
business you don't overlook anything.

The thin galoot outside Gristede's had taken a powder
when I got there; that meant we were no longer playing
girls' rules. I hired a hack to Wanamaker's, cut over to

Third, walked up toward Fourteenth. At Twelfth a mink-faced jasper made up as a street cleaner tailed me for a block, drifted into a dairy restaurant. At Thirteenth somebody dropped a sour tomato out of a third-story window, missing me by inches. I doubled back to Wanamakers, hopped a bus up Fifth to Madison Square, and switched to a cab down Fourth, where the secondhand bookshops elbow each other like dirty urchins.

A flabby hombre in a Joe Carbondale rope-knit sweater, whose jowl could have used a shave, quit giggling over *The Heptameron* long enough to tell me he was Lloyd Thursday. His shoebutton eyes became opaque when I asked to see any first editions or incunabula relative to the *Clupea harengus,* or common herring.

"You got the wrong pitch, copper," he snarled. "That stuff is hotter than Pee Wee Russell's clarinet."

"Maybe a sawbuck'll smarten you up," I said. I folded one to the size of a postage stamp, scratched my chin with it. "There's five yards around for anyone who knows why those Smorgasbits of Sigrid Bjornsterne's happened to be pink." His eyes got crafty.

"I might talk for a grand."

"Start dealing." He motioned toward the back. I took a step forward. A second later a Roman candle exploded inside my head and I went away from there. When I came to, I was on the floor with a lump on my sconce the size of a lapwing's egg and big Terry Tremaine of Homicide was bending over me.

"Someone sapped me," I said thickly. "His name was—"

"Webster," grunted Terry. He held up a dog-eared copy of Merriam's Unabridged, "You tripped on a loose board and this fell off a shelf on your think tank."

"Yeah?" I said skeptically. "Then where's Thursday?" He pointed to the fat man lying across a pile of erotica. "He passed out cold when he saw you cave." I covered up, let Terry figure it any way he wanted. I wasn't telling him what cards I held. I was playing it safe until I knew all the angles.

In a seedy pharmacy off Astor Place, a stale Armenian whose name might have been Vulgarian but wasn't dressed my head and started asking questions. I put my knee in his groin and he lost interest. Jerking my head toward the coffee urn, I spent a nickel and the next forty minutes doing some heavy thinking. Then I holed up in a phone booth and dialed a clerk I knew called Little Farvel in a delicatessen store on Amsterdam Avenue. It took a while to get the dope I wanted because the connection was bad and Little Farvel had been dead two years, but we Noonans don't let go easily.

By the time I worked back to the Arbogast Building, via the Weehawken ferry and the George Washington Bridge to cover my tracks, all the pieces were in place. Or so I thought up to the point she came out of the wardrobe holding me between the sights of her ice-blue automatic.

"Reach for the stratosphere, gumshoe." Sigrid Bjornsterne's voice was colder than Horace Greeley and Little Farvel put together, but her clothes were plenty calorific. She wore a forest-green suit of Hockanum woolens, a Knox Wayfarer, and baby crocodile pumps. It was her blouse, though, that made tiny red hairs stand up on my knuckles. Its deep yoke folds, shoulder pads, and shirtband bow could only have been designed by some master craftsman, some Cézanne of the shears.

"Well, Nosy Parker," she sneered, "so you found out how they tinted the herring."

"Sure—grenadine," I said easily. "You knew it all along. And you planned to add a few grains of oxylbutane-cheriphosphate, which turns the same shade of pink in solution, to your husband's portion, knowing it wouldn't show in the post-mortem. Then you'd collect the three hundred *G*'s and join Harry Pestalozzi in Nogales till the heat died down. But you didn't count on me."

"You?" Mockery nicked her full-throated laugh. "What are you going to do about it?"

"This." I snaked the rug out from under her and she went down in a swirl of silken ankles. The bullet whined by me into the ceiling as I vaulted over the desk, pinioned her against the wardrobe.

"Mike." Suddenly all the hatred had drained away and her body yielded to mine. "Don't turn me in. You cared for me—once."

"It's no good, Sigrid. You'd only double-time me again."

"Try me."

"O.K. The shirtmaker who designed your blouse—what's his name?" A shudder of fear went over her; she averted her head. "He's famous on two continents. Come on Sigrid, they're your dice."

"I won't tell you. I can't. It's a secret between this—this department store and me."

"They wouldn't be loyal to you. They'd sell you out fast enough."

"Oh, Mike, you mustn't. You don't know what you're asking."

"For the last time."

"Oh, sweetheart, don't you see?" Her eyes were tragic pools, a cenotaph to lost illusions. "I've got so little. Don't take that away from me. I—I'd never be able to hold up my head in Russeks again."

"Well, if that's the way you want to play it..." There was silence in the room, broken only by Sigrid's choked sob. Then, with a strangely empty feeling, I uncradled the phone and dialed Spring 7-3100.

For an hour after they took her away, I sat alone in the taupe-colored dusk, watching lights come on and a woman in the hotel opposite adjusting a garter. Then I treated my tonsils to five fingers of firewater, jammed on my hat, and made for the anteroom. Birdie was still scowling over her crossword puzzle. She looked up crookedly at me.

"Need me any more tonight?"

"No." I dropped a grand or two in her lap. "Here, buy yourself some stardust."

"Thanks, I've got my quota." For the first time I caught a shadow of pain behind her eyes. "Mike, would—would you tell me something?"

"As long as it isn't clean," I flipped to conceal my bitterness.

"What's an eight-letter word meaning 'sentimental'?"

"Flatfoot, darling," I said, and went out into the rain.

The Most of S. J. Perleman. NY: Simon & Schuster, 1958.

Alan Coren

Doctor No Will See You Now

To be sure, Alan Coren is British. Quite British. So thoroughly British that when he chooses he can become completely incomprehensible to an American. At the same time, Alan Coren is also the author of a series of very funny children's books set in the American Old West. And his checkered past contains *The Peanut Papers*, ostensibly from the pen of Miz Lillian Carter herself. A versatile man, this Alan Coren.

The London *Sunday Times* has called him "arguably the funniest writer in Britain," to which Coren's only comment is "'Arguably' is not a word I would use." His humor is very much in the Benchley/Perelman tradition, often growing topically out of the everyday bizarre events to be found in the newspapers. If he has a recurring theme, it's the British mastery of failure.

41

Coren started writing humor while working for his Ph.D. at Berkeley in the early '60s, a splendid time to begin observing the colonists. He sent off the pieces to *Punch,* the British humor magazine, where he was almost immediately offered a job. He spent a proud career there, rising to the top as editor in 1977.

James Bond, culture-hero, is by far the most famous spy in the world, thanks to the long line of incredibly successful movies based upon Ian Fleming's indestructible hero. (The only movie in the series to fail, ironically, was the spoof of *Casino Royale* written by Woody Allen, after which he resolved never again to give up any control over his movies.) All of Bond's familiar gadgetry and supporting cast are on view in "Doctor No Will See You Now," along with a broad sampling of Coren's typically jaundiced view of British life, a combination more destructive to Mr. Bond than SMERSH or SPECTRE have ever been.

*   *   *

CIA agents who lose the qualities that make good spies are retired at fifty under special pensions, according to testimony yesterday before a House Intelligence Sub-Committee. "A 70-year-old James Bond is kind of hard to imagine," said Republican Senator Sam Stratton.—Herald Tribune

BOND TENSED IN THE DARKNESS, and reached for his teeth.

There was something in the room.

You did not train for fifty-three years without developing that imponderable acuity that lay beyond mere observation. Indeed, you found that as the years went by, this sixth sense came, perforce, to replace the others: these days, he could hear dog-whistles, with or without his batteries in.

At least, he assumed they were dog-whistles. Nobody else seemed to hear them.

The teeth fell exactly to hand, there between the senna and the Algipan on his bedside table. He waited a calculated split-second for the cement to cleave snugly to his palate. It felt good. It should have: it was made for him by Chas. Fillibee of Albermarle Street, the world's premier fixative man. Senior British agents had been going to Fillibee since before the War; he knew their special requirements. When Witherspoon 004 had gone into the London clinic to have his prostate done and the KGB had taken the opportunity to lob an Ostachnikov nuclear mortar into his grape-box, the only thing left intact between Baker Street Station and the Euston underpass had been Witherspoon's upper plate.

Very carefully, Bond slid his hand beneath his pillow and closed it around the ribbed butt of his Walther PPK 9mm Kurz with the custom-enlarged trigger guard by Rinz of Stuttgart which allowed the arthritic knuckle of Bond's forefinger to slide smoothly around the trigger. His other hand took the light switch.

In one smooth, practised move, Bond snapped on the light switch and simultaneously peered around the room.

There was a shadowy, half-familiar figure by the dressing table. Bond fired, twice, the fearful reports cracking back and forth between the walls, and the figure reeled.

"So much," murmured Bond coolly, "for Comrade Nevachevski!"

Miss Moneypenny sat up in bed, her grizzled bun unravelling, her elegant muffler in fetching disarray.

"You silly old sod," she said.

Bond beamed, deafly.

"Yes, wasn't it?" he said. "Inch or so wide, mind, should've been straight between the eyes, but, my God, he didn't even have time to draw!"

"YOU'VE SHOT YOUR WIG-STAND!" shouted Miss Moneypenny. She stuck an ephedrine inhaler in her left nostril, and sucked noisily.

Bond put on his bi-focals.

"Ah," he said. He brightened. "Still a bloody good shot, though, eh?"

"I should cocoa," said Moneypenny. "It ricocheted off the hot-water bottle. God alone knows what it's done to your rubber sheet."

"Bloody hell," said Bond.

He switched the light out again, and lay back. As always, after untoward events, his wheeze was bad, crackling round the room like crumpling cellophane.

"Shall I rub you in?" murmured Moneypenny softly, from her distant cot.

"Don't start," said Bond.

Moneypenny sighed. At sixty-eight, it seemed, her virginity was moving slowly but surely beyond threat.

Bond shuffled nonchalantly into M's office and tossed his hat in a neat arc towards the polished antler. The hat fell in the wastebin. 007 stared at it for a time, and finally decided against picking it up. On the last occasion upon which he had attempted a major stoop, it had taken four osteopaths to unwind him.

"Good morning," said M, "if you're from Maintenance, I'd like you to know that the roller towel is getting harder and harder to tug. I don't know what they're doing with them these days. I think they put something in them at the factory. When I was a lad, you could pull them down between thumb and forefinger. Possibly the KGB has a hand in it. Also, I have great difficulty in pulling the soap off that magnetic thingy."

"It's me, sir," said Bond, "00—"

He frowned.

M stared at him glaucously from nonagenarian eyes.

Bond took off his James Lobb galosh, and removed a slip of paper.

"7," he said. "007."

M trembled suddenly. He tugged at a drawer, but it did not budge.

"I've got a gun in here somewhere," he said. "By God, you'll know it when I find it! You're not 007, you swine, I've known 007 fifty years, he's bright ginger!"

"I shot my wig," said Bond, gloomily.

M relaxed.

"No good getting angry with a wig," he said. "It's only doing its job."

"You sent for me," said Bond.

"In the CIA," murmured M, "I'd have been retired forty years ago. I would have one of those thermal pools with a thing that makes waves in it. I would have my own genito-urinary man coming in on a weekly basis. A TV hanging from the ceiling, mink linings for the cold snap, a hollow cane with Remy Martin in it, a rare dog."

"About this job," said Bond.

M blew his nose, ineptly.

"Usual thing," he said. "MIRV-launching Russian satellite has been brought down by a defecting Albanian inter-galactic tailgunner in the pay of the Irgun Zwei Leomi. As you would expect, it has fallen down inside Vesuvius: crack KGB, CIA, Mafia, Triad, and IRA teams are already racing to the spot. I promised the PM we'd send our best man."

"Oh, good," muttered Bond. "You don't think Snuggley might fit the bill better?"

"003?" said M. "His leg's gone in for its annual service. No, James, it's you—bags of parachuting, ski-ing, scuba-diving, unarmed combat, all that, right up your street."

"Quite," said Bond.

"Pop along and see Charlie in Special Equipment," said M.

"This," said Charlie, "is probably the most advanced truss in the world."

"It's snug," said Bond. "What are all these pockets for?"

"Spare surgical stockings," said Charlie, ticking off his fingers, "international pensions book, collapsible alloy crutches, Sanatogen capsules, arch supports, emergency pee bottle, mittens, underwater deaf-aid, thermal liberty bodice, and a handbell in case you fall over somewhere and can't get up."

"Super," said Bond.

"Also," said Charlie, "we've been over your Morris Traveller and, ha-ha, tarted it up a bit. Apart from the fact that you'll now be able to get it up to fifty-five—"

"Christ!"

"—there's an emergency inertia brake that brings it to a dead stop in the event of the driver having a heart attack, plus two big orange lights on stalks in both wings enabling you to drive it through narrow spaces, a foot-button that throws your window out instantly in the event of nausea, an inflatable antihaemorrhoid ring set in the driver's seat that activates at the first scream, and a $3\times$ magnifying windshield that enables you to read road signs without getting out of the car."

"Fantastic," muttered Bond.

"Good luck, 007," said Charlie, "and good hunting!"

He shook Bond's hand, but gently.

Bond nosed forward out of the roundabout, onto the Dover road.

People hooted.

The Traveller lurched forward, stalled, lurched on again. 007 ground into third gear. He glanced in his mirror, for the tenth time. Somebody was following him. They had been following him since Blackheath, almost two hours ago.

At the next traffic light, Bond got out and walked back.

"I don't sell off the float, grandpa," said the milkman.

"Why have you been following me?" said Bond levelly.

"I got no option, have I?" said the milkman. "First off, we're the only two vehicles doing fifteen miles a wossname, second off, every time I bleeding pull out to overtake, you start wandering all over the road."

"Evasive action," snapped 007. "Don't tell me you weren't trying to force me into the ditch. You're with SMERSH, right?"

The milkman took his cap off.

"It says Unigate on here," he said.

"Ha!" cried Bond, and sprang into a Nakusai karate crouch, his left hand a club, his right fingers a dagger.

The milkman got out and helped him up.

"It's this knee I've got," said Bond.

"Shouldn't be out, old geezer like you," said the milkman. "It's freezing."

Bond laughed one of his short dry laughs. Once, men had gone white at the very sound.

"Be warm enough, soon, eh? I trust you're bound for Vesuvius?"

The milkman looked at him.

"I got Mafeking Crescent to do, and a bulk yoghurt up the telephone exchange," he said, "then I'm off home for *Pebble Mill.*"

"A likely story!" cried Bond. "What's under that moustache, you Chinese bastard?"

007 made a lightning grab at the milkman's upper lip, misjudged the distance, and caught his forefinger in his opponent's mouth. The milkman closed his teeth on Bond's frail knuckle, and the agent fell back into the road. As he lay there, a bus-driver walked up, stood on him absently, and said to the milkman.

"These bleeding lights have gone green twice, sunshine."

"Don't blame me," said the milkman, "this old bugger stuck his hand in my gob."

The bus-driver glanced down.

"It's this ten pounds Christmas bonus they're getting," he said. "It's driving 'em all barmy. They've been smoking on the downstairs deck all morning." He bent down, and hauled Bond upright. "Come on, uncle, I'll see you across to the Whelk & Banjo."

He took Bond into the public bar, and sat him on a stool, and went out again.

Bond took five pills. His hand was shaking, his heart was pounding, there was a tic in his right eye, and his bronchitis was coming back. He ought to get on, it was four clear days to Naples, given that he refused to drive at night and wanted to pop into the clinic at Vitry-le-François for his monthly checkup.

But, then again, was it worth it? The KGB might hit him, the CIA might shout at him if he couldn't keep up, his surgical skis were as yet untested, and as for swimming the Bay of Naples, he had noticed in himself of late an unsettling tendency to sink. Added to all of which, his SMERSH counterpart was a big Balinese stripper fifty years his junior, and he doubted that his current sexual techniques would persuade her to defect, given that he preferred doing it in his herringbone overcoat these days, apart from the fact that he had last performed a mere eight months before and seriously doubted whether his forces were yet in a position to be remustered.

It wasn't a bad pub, all in all, thought Bond. He could write out a report from here, elaborating a bit. After all, what could they expect for fifty quid a week after stoppages?

The barman looked up at Bond's cough.

"What'll it be?" he said.

"I'll have a small Wincarnis," said Bond. He took off his balaclava. "Shaken, not stirred."

The Best of Alan Coren. NY: St. Martin's Press.

Ogden Nash

Don't Guess,
Let Me Tell You

One summer afternoon in 1930, a young advertising copywriter jotted down a couple of lines of verse:

> I sit in an office at 244 Madison Avenue
> And say to myself you have a responsible job, havenue?

and promptly threw them in the wastebasket. The job may have been responsible, but the rhyme was not: certainly the circular file was its appropriate home. Our young hero, however, had second thoughts and retrieved the paper from the trash. Seemingly within minutes of sending it off to *The New Yorker* he was famous.

Nash's whimsical rhymes and phantasmagoric meter are *sui generis,* themselves favorites of parodists. Although his

jingles and couplets are imprinted on American's brains—
yes, he is originator of Candy/Is dandy,/But liquor/Is
quicker—the true Nash style can be best seen in these
opening lines from "Do Sphinxes Think?"

> There is one thing I do not understand,
> Which is how anybody successfully cuts the finger-
>   nails on their right hand,
> Because it is easy to cut your left-hand fingernails, but
>   with your right hand fingernails, why you either
>   have to let them grow ad infinitum,
> Or else bitum.

Mary Roberts Rinehart is most closely associated with
what came to be broadly recognized as the Had-I-But-
Known school of mysteries. In these novels the heroine
behaves with all the common sense of the teenager in a
slasher movie, rushing for no discernible reason into
dangerous situations about which she's already been
warned, saying after the fact, had I but known, the
murders could have been avoided, the murderer caught,
and the plot shortened by 200 pages. What is far less well
known is that it was Ogden Nash who hung the label on the
school, doing so in this very poem.

* * *

PERSONALLY I don't care whether a detective-story writer
    was educated in night school or day school.
So long as they don't belong to the H.I.B.K. school,
The H.I.B.K. being a device to which too many detective-
    story writers are prone;
Namely, the Had I But Known.
Sometimes it is the Had I But Known what grim secret
    lurked behind that smiling exterior I would never have
    set foot within the door;

Sometimes the Had I But Known then what I know now I
could have saved at least three lives by revealing to the
Inspector the conversation I heard through that for-
tuitous hole in the floor.

Had I But Known narrators are the ones who hear a
stealthy creak at midnight in the tower where the body
lies, and, instead of locking their door or arousing the
drowsy policeman posted outside their room, sneak
off by themselves to the tower and suddenly they hear
a breath exhaled behind them,

And they have no time to scream, they know nothing else
till the men from the D.A.'s office come in next
morning and find them.

Had I But Known-ers are quick to assume the prerogatives
of the Deity,

For they will suppress evidence that doesn't suit their
theories with appalling spontaneity,

And when the killer is finally trapped into a confession by
some elaborate device of the Had I But Known-ers
some hundred pages later than if they hadn't held
their knowledge aloof,

Why they say Why Inspector I knew all along it was he but
I couldn't tell you, you would have laughed at me
unless I had absolute proof.

Would you like for your library a nice detective story which
I am sorry to say I didn't rent but owns?

I wouldn't have bought it had I but known it was impreg-
nated with Had I But Knowns.

Ogden Nash. *The Face Is Familiar*. Boston: Little Brown, 1940.

Ira Wallach

Me, the Judge

Parodies of current fads are often last year's news, which may be why parodists sometimes seem to have the lifespans of pet rocks. Like Corey Ford and Christopher Ward, Ira Wallach had a hot couple of years publishing an astounding number of parodies, after which he pulled himself out of the literary gutter, dusted himself off, and made some real money writing novels, plays, and screenplays.

His 1951 collection, *Hopalong-Freud and Other Modern Literary Characters* was followed a year later by *Hopalong-Freud Rides Again: Another Literary Ambush*. Like Hopalong Cassidy himself (and maybe even Freud, judging by some of the books on him lately), many of Wallach's targets are as dead as the passenger pigeon. (Give yourself a prize—or possibly a cane and walker—if you remember *Woman, the Lost Sex, How I Raised Myself from Failure to Success in Selling,* or *Vedanta for the Western World*, all presumably hot topics in the early '50s.)

The hottest of the hot in those fun-loving Truman years was Mickey Spillane's Mike Hammer, that lovable refugee from Krafft-Ebing, whose sometimes literally gut-busting epics of sex and blood and blood and sex gave him at one time seven of the top fifteen best-selling paperback novels in history. Modern authors may be racier and gorier than anything dreamt of in the post-war era, but Spillane was a passenger pigeon worth the plucking when Wallach blasted out this two-fisted, two-gunned, and too much parody of his *I, the Jury*.

* * *

PUBLISHER'S PREFACE

"I'm going to cut valentines out of your
large intestine!"

Pete Rivet believed in justice. When the killer struck, Pete swore he'd shoot him down, right through the gut, with a slug as big as a 14-ounce sinker. Then, when the killer was lying there with a slug in his belly, Pete swore he'd kick in his teeth. Then he'd jump on his face. Then he'd get a hacksaw and saw the body into parts.

Then he'd jump on the parts. Then he'd smash the teeth on the hacksaw. Then he'd work over that louse of a hardware dealer who sold him a hacksaw with smashed teeth.

When the suspects piled up, including passionate Martha Emery, passionate Louise Higgleston, and passionate Natalie Wallace, Pete knew this wasn't for mouthpieces and judges and juries. It was up to Pete to keep law and order.

Of *Me, the Judge*, the *Houston Blade* commented, "At last! A writer who knows how to fill in the gaps between blood and sex with blood and sex!" Echoing this praise, a reviewer in the *Chicago Times-Union* wrote, "Pete Rivet is something new in detectives. He is a sadistic, degenerate idiot." These, and other enthusiastic comments, have made *Me, the Judge* a favorite with discriminating readers everywhere.

MODERN CLASSICS, INC.

I.

I WALKED INTO THE ROOM. The body lay in the closet, feet sticking out. Matt Abel looked at me. Mat is a smart cop. "An .88," Matt said.

On the couch sat a girl. Even with her shoulders heaving with sobs I could see she was beautiful.

"Martha Emery," Matt explained. "They were going to get married."

"Poor kid," I murmured. Then I suddenly felt like I was burning up with hate. God, how I hated that killer! Nick Jenkins was my pal, my buddy. Straightest guy that ever lived. I'd grown up with Nick. Together we'd planned to smash some guy's teeth down his throat. It was Nick who taught me how to shove a knife in a mug up and sideways instead of down and straight. Everybody loved Nick.

I stood there looking at what was left of him. "Nick," I said, "It's too late for you to do anything about this. The reason for this is because you are dead, Nick. But listen to me anyway, Nick. I'm going to make you a promise, Nick. I'm going to find the killer, Nick. And when I find him I'm going to let him have it. Right in the belly button, Nick."

I bowed my head out of respect for the dead.

"Take it easy, Pete." It was Matt Abel's voice.

"I'm tired of taking it easy."

"I want the killer," Matt said.

"Nothing doing, Matt. No judge and jury this time. Sometimes those trials drag on three weeks. Sometimes

they even let the guy go because he's innocent. But that
isn't going to happen this time. I'm going to get the killer,
innocent or guilty, and when I do, I'm going to saw off his
head, crack his ribs, jump on his neck, smash his Adam's
apple, beat in his nose, tear off his ears, pull out his hair,
bend back his fingers, twist off his toenails, and shatter his
kneecap. But before I do this I'm going to work him over
with a rusty knife. I'm like that, Matt. I want a clean and
decent America, a place where our kids can grow and sniff
the good fresh air."

Matt sighed. He knew when he was licked.

2.

Matt and the other cops left. I stayed to look around.
Martha, poor kid, was still crying. She said, "Excuse me,"
and she went into the next room. When she came back she
was wearing a cheesecloth negligee that buttoned down the
front. I could see the womanly rippling muscles underneath and the fine wide breasts that fought the negligee to
be free. She sat down on the couch and cut off the buttons.
The negligee fell open. She didn't bother to close it. Huba
huba.

I went over to her. In a moment I felt her soft wet mouth
against mine. She held me so tight it hurt. She was trying
to get closer, closer. "Did Nick have any enemies?" I asked.

"Not that I know of," she said. God, she was beautiful.

"Anything strike you as unusual about him last week?"

"Nothing," she moaned, "except that he said he had to
spend the weekend at the Higglestons in Long Island."

I pushed her away from me and straightened my tie.
"Got to go to Long Island," I said.

She held her arms toward me.

"Not now, baby," I said. "I want it to be beautiful. This
would spoil everything."

I left. Behind me I heard Martha beating her head against the wall in rage and exasperation. I chuckled.

3.

Jane Higgleston was society. She was in her sixties, and she gave some of the real swank shindigs on the island. Only I knew that Jane Higgleston ran a string of whore houses and also had her finger in the dope trade and the numbers racket.

The Higgleston estate was the flashiest thing on the Island. I drove up at 80 m.p.h., braked the wreck in front of the door, and jumped out. The butler opened the door. I pulled out my .45 and laid open his cheek with the butt end. You could see his molars with his mouth closed. "Now can I come in?" I asked.

I found Jane Higgleston sitting in her wheel chair. I flashed my badge.

"Well, Mr. Rivet, what can I do for you?" she asked.

"Tell me how you first met Nick Jenkins."

"I never met Nick Jenkins," she said. She was a cool one, all right. But I knew how to handle that. When she wasn't looking I came up with my fist and it landed in her midriff right up to the wrist. She slipped to the floor with a groan. I took the old biddy's cane and beat her across the nape of the neck. "Now maybe you'll talk," I said.

"All right," she groaned. "How do you want me to have met Nick Jenkins?"

"You met Nick Jenkins three years ago at the community bake in Scarsdale. He entered his cocaine muffins. They won the prize over your opium dumplings. You hated him ever since, but you didn't kill him. Now snarl."

She snarled, and I let her have one in the eye for good measure.

When I turned something stopped me short. It was a

woman. But when I say it was a woman, I don't say
anything. She was a fine shade of tan, and under her dress
I could see the light delicate muscles ripple. She had fine
wide shoulders and handsome breasts that struck out
against the jacket of her smart suit. Huba huba.

"I am Louise Higgleston," she said. "Pardon me one
moment." She left the room. When she returned she was
dressed only in a pair of peach-fuzz panties. She lay down
on the couch and beckoned.

I went over, my blood on fire. In a moment I felt her lips
against mine, her body pressing hard. I could hardly
breathe. The blood was hammering in my head. "Take me
now," she gasped.

"Where was Martha Emery the night before Nick
Jenkins met his death?"

"She was at a cock fight with the Governor and Natalie
Wallace," she murmured, fighting to get closer.

I stood up and straightened my tie. There's a time for
everything.

"Don't go," she begged.

"I want you," I said, "but it's got to be beautiful. Let's not
spoil everything."

I rushed out, pausing only long enough to shoot the
butler.

4.

A bullet *zinged* by me as I started driving out. I dashed
out of the wreck and charged back. In a moment I saw
what had happened. Louise Higgleston lay on the floor, a
bullet in her gut. I turned the corpse over with my toe.

I looked around. There was no exit except for the front
door and the side doors. The window ledge was too narrow
for the killer to have escaped that way. I tested the
chandelier. I couldn't swing from the chandelier to the

kitchen. The fire place was blocked. There was no room between the dining room table and the wall. How did the killer leave? Why did Natalie Wallace conceal her visit to the cock fight from her mother? Was the Governor involved with the Breslin gang? What did Nick do that year he spent in Bryn Mawr? Why did the Dean ask him to leave? Somewhere a link was missing. I had to get hold of that link.

I drove to a luncheonette to have a bite and think. The waitress came over. She was wearing a smock with no buttons. It hung open. She had nothing on underneath. Huba huba. "Tunafish on white," I said.

"Butter and lettuce?"

I grabbed her by the collar of the smock and twisted till her face turned blue. She slumped to the floor, gasping, "Take me now!" I broke a pitcher of water over her head. She came to. I yanked her up by the ear and let her have it over the side of the head with my .45. "Did I say butter and lettuce?" I snarled.

I drove to the apartment. No one was home. I jimmied open the door, sat down in an arm chair, and released the safety on the .45.

In a few minutes she came in. She was cool, all right. I'll have to hand her that. She started to speak.

"It's no use, Natalie," I said. "I didn't realize it was you till I found the one little link. There was no exit from the Higgleston place. That means you didn't leave."

(She was coming toward me now, her nostrils flaring, her beautiful breasts scrimmaging with a nylon blouse.)

"If you didn't leave, that means you were there. And if you were there, that means you shot Louise Higgleston because she knew of your connections with Danny Devine."

(Her lips were open now, and they were flaring, too. I couldn't look. I had to go on talking.)

"Then I realized that you had cooked Nick's cocaine

muffins, enabling him to receive first prize. Then you shot him. Why? So you could get in good with Martha Emery and run the racket from her end."

(Slowly she walked toward me, undulating rapidly. I felt my heart pounding. I knew I'd never see anything as undulant again in my life.)

"A jury wouldn't convict you on my evidence. I know that. But I convict you. Now."

(She was fumbling with the zipper on her blouse. The zipper made the soft enticing zippy sound that passionate women make when they zip their zippers. Huba huba.)

"It's no use, Natalie," I said, levelling my .45 at her belly.

"Wait," she murmured. "You can't shoot me yet."

The roar and smoke of the .45 cut her off. She grabbed her gut and looked at me in amazement. Then she sank to the floor.

"Pete," she gasped, "you shot me! Fully dressed!"

I started out. In the hall I met my publisher. "Pete," he said in his cultured accents, "you shot her fully dressed?"

"Yes," I said. "I was in a hurry. I want a clean decent America."

"Pete," he said, "go back in, undress her, and shoot her again."

After I did it, I saw Matt Abel standing in the doorway. "Some day, Pete," he said, "you're going to overreach yourself. She was a taxpayer."

Ira Wallach. *Hopalong-Freud Rides Again.* NY: Henry Schuman, 1952.

Stephen Leacock

Maddened by Mystery: or, The Defective Detective

Let's face it, the best humorists are brats, young wise guys and gals with chips on their shoulders. Most of the pieces in this book were written by writers in their twenties.

And then there's Stephen Leacock, who was a staid professor of Political Economy when, at the age of forty, he tried sending a publisher a collection of humorous essays. The publisher sent them right back. As an economist Leacock knew exactly what to do next. He published them himself.

Most of the time, the story would end right there, with the professor poorer but wiser. But this particular book, which Leacock called *Literary Lapses,* started off with "My Financial Career," soon to become one of the most reprinted pieces of humor of the century. The book quickly sold out, launching Leacock on a long career as a humorist of international renown.

Leacock's fine sense of nonsense and his favorite character, a sort of average man befuddled and beset by the everyday world, can be seen, perfected, in the best of Robert Benchley (who once said, by the way, "I have enjoyed Leacock's work so much that I have written everything he ever wrote—anywhere from one to five years after him.").

Leacock's second book, *Nonsense Novels*, contained a whole series of parodies of the popular literature of his day. Few of the genres still live; the parodies do. Here is the famous line, Lord Ronald "flung himself upon his horse and rode madly off in all directions." Here is "'Q.' A Psychic Pstory of the Psupernatural." And here Leacock skewers Sherlock Holmes as the Great Detective. This is an early parody, from 1911 in fact, but Holmes was already world famous, with each and every one of his idiosyncracies known in loving detail to his millions of fans. Much reprinted, "Maddened by Mystery" is still the classic Holmes parody and I had no choice but to include it in this book. After all, I too owe Leacock a debt: I stole the title of this celebratory volume from him.

* * *

THE GREAT DETECTIVE sat in his office.

He wore a long green gown and half a dozen secret badges pinned to the outside of it.

Three or four pairs of false whiskers hung on a whisker-stand beside him.

Goggles, blue spectacles and motor glasses lay within easy reach.

He could completely disguise himself at a second's notice.

Half a bucket of cocaine and a dipper stood on a chair at his elbow.

His face was absolutely impenetrable.

A pile of cryptograms lay on the desk. The Great Detective hastily tore them open one after the other, solved them, and threw them down the cryptogram-shute at his side.

There was a rap at the door.

The Great Detective hurriedly wrapped himself in a pink domino, adjusted a pair of false black whiskers and cried,

"Come in."

His secretary entered. "Ha," said the detective, "it is you!"

He laid aside the disguise.

"Sir," said the young man in intense excitement, "a mystery has been committed!"

"Ha!" said the Great Detective, his eye kindling, "is it such as to completely baffle the police of the entire continent?"

"They are so completely baffled with it," said the secretary, "that they are lying collapsed in heaps; many of them have committed suicide."

"So," said the detective, "and is the mystery one that is absolutely unparalleled in the whole recorded annals of the London police?"

"It is."

"And I suppose," said the detective, "that it involves names which you would scarcely dare to breathe, at least without first using some kind of atomiser or throat-gargle."

"Exactly."

"And it is connected, I presume, with the highest diplomatic consequences, so that if we fail to solve it England will be at war with the whole world in sixteen minutes?"

His secretary, still quivering with excitement, again answered yes.

"And finally," said the Great Detective, "I presume that it was committed in broad daylight, in some place as the entrance of the Bank of England, or in the cloak-room of the House of Commons, and under the very eyes of the police?"

"Those," said the secretary, "are the very conditions of the mystery."

"Good," said the Great Detective, "now wrap yourself in this disguise, put on these brown whiskers and tell me what it is."

The secretary wrapped himself in a blue domino with lace insertions, then, bending over, he whispered in the ear of the Great Detective:

"The Prince of Wurttemberg has been kidnapped."

The Great Detective bounded from his chair as if he had been kicked from below.

A prince stolen! Evidently a Bourbon! The scion of one of the oldest families in Europe kidnapped. Here was a mystery indeed worthy of his analytical brain.

His mind began to move like lightning.

"Stop!" he said, "how do you know this?"

The secretary handed him a telegram. It was from the Prefect of Police of Paris. It read: "The Prince of Wurttemberg stolen. Probably forwarded to London. Must have him here for the opening day of Exhibition. £1,000 reward."

So! The Prince had been kidnapped out of Paris at the very time when his appearance at the International Exposition would have been a political event of the first magnitude.

With the Great Detective to think was to act, and to act was to think. Frequently he could do both together.

"Wire to Paris for a description of the Prince."

The secretary bowed and left.

At the same moment there was a slight scratching at the door.

A visitor entered. He crawled stealthily on his hands and knees. A hearthrug thrown over his head and shoulders disguised his identity.

He crawled to the middle of the room.

Then he rose.

Great Heaven!

It was the Prime Minister of England.

"You!" said the detective.

"Me," said the Prime Minister.

"You have come in regard to the kidnapping of the Prince of Wurttenberg?"

The Prime Minister started.

"How do you know?" he said.

The Great Detective smiled his inscrutable smile.

"Yes," said the Prime Minister. "I will use no concealment. I am interested, deeply interested. Find the Prince of Wurttemberg, get him safe back to Paris and I will add £500 to the reward already offered. But listen," he said impressively as he left the room, "see to it that no attempt is made to alter the marking of the prince, or to clip his tail."

So! To clip the Prince's tail! The brain of the Great Detective reeled. So! a gang of miscreants had conspired to—but no! the thing was not possible.

There was another rap at the door.

A second visitor was seen. He wormed his way in, lying almost prone upon his stomach, and wriggling across the floor. He was enveloped in a long purple cloak. He stood up and peeped over the top of it.

Great Heaven!

It was the Archbishop of Canterbury!

"Your Grace!" exclaimed the detective in amazement—"pray do not stand, I beg you. Sit down, lie down, anything rather than stand."

The Archbishop took off his mitre and laid it wearily on the whisker-stand.

"You are here in regard to the Prince of Wurttenberg."

The Archbishop started and crossed himself. Was the man a magician?

"Yes," he said, "much depends on getting him back. But I have only come to say this: my sister is desirous of seeing you. She is coming here. She has been extremely indiscreet and her fortune hangs upon the Prince. Get him back to Paris or I fear she will be ruined."

The Archbishop regained his mitre, uncrossed himself, wrapped his cloak about him, and crawled stealthily out on his hands and knees, purring like a cat.

The face of the Great Detective showed the most profound sympathy. It ran up and down in furrows. "So," he muttered, "the sister of the Archbishop, the Countess of Dashleigh!" Accustomed as he was to the life of the aristocracy, even the Great Detective felt that there was here intrigue of more than customary complexity.

There was a loud rapping at the door.

There entered the Countess of Dashleigh. She was all in furs.

She was the most beautiful woman in England. She strode imperiously into the room. She seized a chair imperiously and seated herself on it, imperial side up.

She took off her tiara of diamonds and put it on the tiara-holder beside her and uncoiled her boa of pearls and put it on the pearlstand.

"You have come," said the Great Detective, "about the Prince of Wurttemberg."

"Wretched little pup!" said the Countess of Dashleigh in disgust.

So! A further complication! Far from being in love with the Prince, the Countess denounced the young Bourbon as a pup!

"You are interested in him, I believe."

"Interested!" said the Countess. "I should rather say so. Why, I bred him!"

"You which?" gasped the Great Detective, his usually impassive features suffused with a carmine blush.

"I bred him," said the Countess, "and I've got £10,000 upon his chances, so no wonder I want him him back in Paris. Only listen," she said, "if they've got hold of the Prince and cut his tail or spoiled the markings of his stomach it would be far better to have him quietly put out of the way here."

The Great Detective reeled and leaned up against the side of the room. So! The cold-blooded admission of the beautiful woman for the moment took away his breath! Herself the mother of the young Bourbon, misallied with one of the greatest families of Europe, staking her fortune on a Royalist plot, and yet with so instinctive a knowledge of European politics as to know that any removal of the hereditary birth-marks of the Prince would forfeit for him the sympathy of the French populace.

The Countess resumed her tiara.

She left.

The secretary re-entered.

"I have three telegrams from Paris," he said, "they are completely baffling."

He handed over the first telegram.

It read:

"The Prince of Wurttemberg has a long, wet snout, broad ears, very long body, and short hind legs."

The Great Detective looked puzzled.

He read the second telegram.

"The Prince of Wurttemberg is easily recognized by his deep bark."

And then the third.

"The Prince of Wurteemberg can be recognized by the patch of white hair across the centre of his back."

The two men looked at one another. The mystery was maddening, impenetrable.

The Great Detective spoke.

"Give me my domino," he said. "These clues must be

followed up," then pausing, while his quick brain analysed and summed up the evidence before him— "a young man," he muttered, "evidently young since described as a 'pup,' with a long, wet snout (ha! addicted obviously to drinking), a streak of white hair across his back (a first sign of the results of his abandoned life)—yes, yes," he continued, "with this clue I shall find him easily."

The Great Detective rose.

He wrapped himself in a long black cloak with white whiskers and blue spectacles attached.

Completely disguised, he issued forth.

He began the search.

For four days he visited every corner of London.

He entered every saloon in the city. In each of them he drank a glass of rum. In some of them he assumed the disguise of a sailor. In others he entered as a soldier. Into others he penetrated as a clergyman. His disguise was perfect. Nobody paid any attention to him as long as he had the price of a drink.

The search proved fruitless.

Two young men were arrested under suspicion of being the Prince, only to be released.

The identification was incomplete in each case.

One had a long wet snout but no hair on his back.

The other had hair on his back but couldn't bark.

Neither of them was the young Bourbon.

The Great Detective continued his search.

He stopped at nothing.

Secretly, after nightfall, he visited the home of the Prime Minister. He examined it from top to bottom. He measured all the doors and windows. He took up the flooring. He inspected the plumbing. He examined the furniture. He found nothing.

With equal secrecy he penetrated into the palace of the Archbishop. He examined it from top to bottom. Disguised as a choir-boy he took part in the offices of the church. He found nothing.

Still undismayed, the Great Detective made his way into the home of the Countess of Dashleigh. Disguised as a housemaid, he entered the service of the Countess.

Then at last the clue came which gave him a solution of the mystery.

On the wall of the Countess' boudoir was a large framed engraving.

It was a portrait.

Under it was a printed legend.

THE PRINCE OF WURTTEMBERG

The portrait was that of a Dachshund.

The long body, the broad ears, the unclipped tail, the short hind legs—all was there.

In the fraction of a second the lightning mind of the Great Detective had penetrated the whole mystery.

THE PRINCE WAS A DOG!!!!

Hastily throwing a domino over his housemaid's dress, he rushed to the street. He summoned a passing hansom, and in a few moments was at his house.

"I have it," he gasped to his secretary, "the mystery is solved. I have pieced it together. By sheer analysis I have reasoned it out. Listen—hind legs, hair on back, wet snout, pup—eh, what? does that suggest nothing to you?"

"Nothing," said the secretary; "it seems perfectly hopeless."

The Great Detective, now recovered from his excitement, smiled faintly.

"It means simply this, my dear fellow. The Prince of Wurttemburg is a dog, a prize Dachshund. The Countess of Dashleigh bred him, and he is worth some £25,000 in addition to the prize of £10,000 offered at the Paris dog show. Can you wonder that—"

At that moment the Great Detective was interrupted by the scream of a woman.

"Great Heaven!"

The Countess of Dashleigh dashed into the room.

Her face was wild.

Her tiara was in disorder.

Her pearls were dripping all over the place.

She wrung her hands and moaned.

"They have cut his tail," she gasped, "and taken all the hair off his back. What can I do? I am undone! !"

"Madame," said the Great Detective, calm as bronze, "do yourself up. I can save you yet."

"You!"

"Me!"

"How?"

"Listen. This is how. The Prince was to have been shown at Paris."

The Countess nodded.

"Your fortune was staked on him?"

The Countess nodded again.

"The dog was stolen, carried to London, his tail cut and his marks disfigured."

Amazed at the quiet penetration of the Great Detective, the Countess kept on nodding and nodding.

"And you are ruined?"

"I am," she gasped, and sank down on the floor in a heap of pearls.

"Madame," said the Great Detective, "all is not lost."

He straightened himself up to his full height. A look of inflinchable unflexibility flickered over his features.

The honour of England, the fortune of the most beautiful woman in England was at stake.

"I will do it," he murmured.

"Rise, dear lady," he continued. "Fear nothing. I WILL IMPERSONATE THE DOG! ! !"

That night the Great Detective might have been seen on the deck of the Calais packet boat with his secretary. He was on his hands and knees in a long black cloak, and his secretary had him on a short chain.

He barked at the waves exultingly and licked the secretary's hand.

"What a beautiful dog," said the passengers.

The disguise was absolutely complete.

The Great Detective had been coated over with mucilage to which dog hairs had been applied. The markings on his back were perfect. His tail, adjusted with an automatic coupler, moved up and down responsive to every thought. His deep eyes were full of intelligence.

Next day he was exhibited in the Dachshund class at the International show.

He won all hearts.

"*Quel beau chien!*" cried the French people.

"*Ach! was ein Dog!*" cried the Spanish.

The Great Detective took the first prize!

The fortune of the Countess was saved.

Unfortunately as the Great Detective had neglected to pay the dog tax, he was caught and destroyed by the dog-catchers. But that is, or course, quite outside of the present narrative, and is only mentioned as an odd fact in conclusion.

Stephen Leacock. *Nonsense Novels.* NY: Dodd, Mead, 1961 (reprint).

Henry Beard

The Big Recall

Nothing destroys a writer's ego more than to be continually identified with his juvenilia. The problem, in Beard's case, is that the stuff was so damn good. The latest in a series of campus humor magazine heroes (following Benchley, Ford, Perelman, and Thurber, among many others) he was on the staff of the *Harvard Lampoon* during its heyday of the *Playboy* and *Life* magazine parodies. When the latter lost money (who in the *Lampoon*'s audience cared about *Life* magazine in 1968 anyway?), he and Doug Kenney more than recouped their losses by writing *Bored of the Rings,* a Tolkein parody that sold a mere 750,000 copies. The two of them then founded the *National Lampoon,* of which Beard was editor during the year or two the magazine could be considered legendary. In and around those years, the magazine's pages were filled with another string of note-perfect parodies out of Beard's typewriter.

The latter-day Beard no longer gives out interviews on his salad days or on much else, but his publishing record since then displays a fine eye for hip whimsy. His was the hand behind *Miss Piggy's Guide to Life* and *Latin for All Occasions,* and his acidic definitions have made *Fishing, Sailing, Cooking, Golfing, Skiing,* and *Gardening* big sellers. Most recently he collaborated with other NatLamp refugees to produce a giant collection of parodies, *The Book of Sequels.*

None of these show off his talents like his extraordinary mystery parodies. Usually his parodies were merciless skewerings, with targets as diverse as Mickey Spillane and the hardy Boys left quivering in the dust. His brilliant and Raymond Chandlersque "The Big Recall," however, is more of a salute from one master of the metaphor to another. Here the true villain is General Motors, who had just made the idiotic move of placing a private detective on Ralph Nader's trail to dig up dirt on the ascetic consumer crusader. By making Nader his hardboiled hero in a shoddily-built world, Beard creates social commentary as acute as any of Chandler's and as funny as anything else he's written.

* * *

IT WAS SIX-THIRTY ON A MONDAY, and the late autumn sun was going through its daily dramatization outside my fifth-story window, sinking through the murky Washington air like that pearl in the bottle of Prell. For a quarter of an hour the sky was a grifter's dream, with good, bright television colors and no law that said you had to run a line underneath saying "Hydrocarbons and sulfides added to enhance color." When you took a deep breath, it was like being back in the chem lab when they showed you how to make the yellow stuff turn into green stuff and bubble, and afterwards, when they opened you up to find out why you came up shy a couple of decades on your three score and ten, your lungs were a dead ringer for the Before picture in a Midas muffler ad, but for fifteen minutes on a good day, it's almost worth it. That leaves only 1,425 minutes when it isn't. They say the air is one thing you can't bottle and sell, but tell that to the people who live next to an air freshener factory and have to buy air freshener because the air smells like someone has been wearing it to work for a week.

I was sitting in my swivel chair and staring at the telephone, and I was thinking how much I looked like the washer repairman in that Maytag commercial who never gets calls because Maytag washers never break down. I was wondering why the Naval Observatory doesn't replace its cesium clocks with something really reliable like a couple of that company's legendary top-loaders, when I heard a pair of high heels coming down the corridor, doing the timpani score from the *Lt. Kije Suite.*

They stopped, and then a hand rapped on the pebbleglass outer door that has "Ralph Nader, Investigations" on it in flaking black paint, and then the buzzer sounded. I wasn't expecting anyone, and I was pretty sure it wasn't the Avon lady come to sell me $4 worth of scented skin irritant in a bottle shaped like a shoe.

I picked up my feet off the desk where I had left them an hour before. They were asleep, probably dreaming of spending their days in fifty-dollar wing-tips instead of cheap Weejuns. I hobbled through the connecting door and across the faded cloth vomit mat that has been auditioning for the role of carpet in my outer office for the past four years. I opened the door.

The pair of high heels were just outside. In them were a nice pair of ankles, and a nice pair of legs, and a nice pair of knees, and from there on up, past a miniskirt that was at least as large as a wildlife commemorative, she'd been dealt a lot of nice pairs, right up to the nice pair of blue eyes she was watching me add up her nice pairs with.

"Well," she said, "do I pass the Starkist test, or is it back to Charlie the Tuna?" She had that pleasant, half-happy, half-surprised kind of voice Hollywood housewives use when they find they've picked the towels washed in Wisk.

"Come in," I said, wondering if this was going to be one of those cases where the client has all the good lines.

I led her into the inner office, and held a chair for her, and helped her fasten the seat belt.

"What the hell is this for?" she asked.

"Seventy-five percent of all accidents happen in the home or office," I answered, settling back in my swivel chair. It didn't have a belt. When John Beresford Tipton gives me the nod, I'm going to have one of those air bags that inflate in a tenth of a second installed under the desk, but meanwhile I've got an agreement with myself that if anything happens to me on my own ground, I won't sue.

"Where's yours?" she asked.

Every now and then you'll get a setup like that, right out of the blue, and when you've been in business for as long as I have, you don't let it go by.

"I've got an agreement with myself that if anything happens to me on my own ground, I won't sue," I said.

She laughed. I listened for the little chime that tells you a lipstick mark is going to appear on your forehead, but all I got was a metallic raspberry from the one-armed bandit the Bell Telephone Company maintains in my office for when I fell like gambling a few dimes on the spin of a dial to try to beat the one-hundred-to-one odds against getting any seven-digit number on the first try.

"Nader here," I said into the phone. Then I said, "Name this tune," and whistled "Taps."

"What's the gag, Nader?" Whoever it was was speaking through a handkerchief, but, with all the taps, it sounded like the Brain from Planet Arous addressing the people of Earth from orbit around Jupiter.

"Most people don't know this," I said, "but there's this juicy stuff in telephone wires that a lot of people go for.

Right now the sap's running, and there's a lot of little men running around sticking little things in the trunk lines to drain off this stuff...."

"Okay, okay, I get it," said the voice. "Now listen and listen good. There's a dame there. If you know what's good for you, you'll kiss her off. If you don't, you'll be in circulation about as long as a can of Bon Vivant. Get me?"

I had recently stumbled on a novel method of sexual self-gratification, and I wanted to pass it on to the caller as a friendly gesture in return for this advice, but he had hung up, and the anthropologists who are preserving all my phone conversations as a priceless source of folk humor had heard it already, and anyway, there was a lady in the room.

"Who was that?" said the lady in the room.

"My daily death threat. It's a sort of service. I pay $2.50 a month and someone at the agency calls up and tells me they're going to kill me. It keeps me on my toes." I didn't tell her she was included in today's call.

She had that look people get when you tell them the ingredients of a frankfurter after a weenie roast. "That's terrible," she said.

I didn't say anything.

"Mr. Nader," she said, "I'm in trouble and I don't know what to do."

"You can start by telling me your name."

"Penny," she said. "Penny Stallworth." It sounded like a deceptive label, and maybe it looked like I was having difficulty swallowing it, because she gave me her hand for a chaser. It was the kind of hand you expected to find on the other end of a leash from a dog that barked in five languages and did its duty in little linen envelopes and mailed them to the Superintendent of Sanitation. I gave it back and it went right to the other hand and told it about the wart on my index finger and the crooked thumb I got trying to trepan a running power-mower when I was eight.

"What can I do for you, Miss, or is it Mrs., Stallworth?"

"It's Mrs.," she said and the hand I had met went inside a purse made from the skin of an animal that there are about enough left of to field a baseball team as long as you didn't mind them putting in a couple of raccoons as pinch hitters. When it came out, it was holding an envelope. She passed it across the desk.

I opened it and took out a half-dozen color photographs taken with a Polaroid. They all showed the same thing: a red 1970 Chevrolet Camaro that probably couldn't go much faster than the speed of sound, and if anything went wrong, they'd have to help you out with a high-pressure hose. One of the views showed the front end and a D.C. license plate. In the background of a couple of the shots was a house that looked like the Six Months Later picture in one of those articles in *Better Homes and Gardens* that tells how a couple from Baltimore turned a rundown chicken shed into a villa with only $650 and some old gold bricks they found in a well. One of the pictures showed a distinguished-looking man who was taking a break between poses for the Abercrombe & Fitch catalogue. He had a metallic look; steel-gray hair, iron jaw, copper complexion. He probably also had a tin ear and a heart of lead, but I was just guessing.

"Is this your car?" I asked.

"Yes, it is," she said, "or was, until last week when a friend of mine took it back to the dealer to get a bumper fixed. It vanished."

"It sounds like you should be talking to the dealer, or to the police."

"I talked to the dealer. A man named Spinetti, at Beltway Buick. Mr. Nader, the car had great sentimental value."

"Sentimental value?"

"The friend of mine vanished with it."

"The man in the picture?" I held up the photograph.

"No. The man in the picture is my husband."

"I see."

"And I'm sure you also see why I can't go to the police. Anyway, Larry didn't steal it."

I said I saw why she couldn't go to the police but that the kind of investigation she had in mind wasn't in my line.

"You mean you go in more for finding old derby winners in hot dogs." I let that go by.

"I'm sorry," she said. "I guess I'm upset. But this is in your line. You see, Larry, Larry Rendall, that's my friend, or was,"—there was a catch in her voice but I could have gotten one just like it for 39 cents in any hardware store in town—"was something of a car nut. He raced stock cars off and on during the summer at the local tracks. Anyway, he used to enjoy fooling around with my car."

"The Camaro?"

"Yes. He always wanted me to let him race it, and of course I wouldn't, but he still liked to tune it or whatever it is. He was always talking about compression ratios and torque and things. Then last week he took it entirely apart, and put it back together. That was Monday. That night when I saw him, he was very excited, joking around and everything. He showed me a picture he had taken of the car in a heap of little pieces, just to tease me, and then he gave me this." This time the hand brought out a plastic bag and emptied it on my desk. When it was finished, there was a little heap of broken metal shards.

"He said it was a motor bolt or something, that he had taken it out of the engine and that just by chance he had hit it with a hammer and there was something wrong with the alloy because it broke like a piece of clay. He said it was our ticket to freedom."

"Freedom?"

"He wanted me to get a divorce from my husband and marry him, but neither of us has any money, and I for one didn't plan to live like a pauper. Anyway, Larry said that little gismo was a defective part, and he said he had checked and there was one in just about every Chevrolet made in the last seven years, maybe ten million cars in all, and that GM would pay quite a lot to keep it quiet. He said if anyone found out, it would cost them millions to recall all the cars and millions more in damage suits, because it must have caused thousands of accidents. I thought he was crazy."

I wasn't doing any talking.

"I didn't hear from Larry again until Friday morning when I got a call from him. He was excited and said he had talked to someone, I think he said Spinetti, and it looked like they were going to come up with a lot of money. He wanted to borrow the car. I told him he could, but I asked him to drop it off at Beltway Buick when he was finished. I couldn't see him because I had to have lunch in town with my husband. Larry had his own set of keys to the car. That's the last I saw of him. We were supposed to meet at his place after he got finished working Friday night. I went there and I rang the bell for about a half an hour but there wasn't any answer."

"Did he tell anyone else about finding the defect?"

"Not that I know of."

"Did he say where he was going to meet Spinetti?"

"No." She slumped a little. "I'm not being very much help, am I?"

"Does your husband know about this?"

"No. As far as he knows, I drove the car to the dealer and took a cab into the city."

"What does Spinetti say?"

"That neither Larry nor the car ever showed up."

"What happens when you have to explain where the car is, and your husband finds out you didn't drive it over?"

She smiled. "I'll play silly blonde and tell him I was late and so I hired a nice-looking boy on the street to drive it over for me for five dollars and then I didn't tell him because he would have been angry with me for being so foolish because that's how cars get stolen, and he was right, because that's just what must have happened." While she was talking, her face assumed a pout and her voice broke a little, and I had to pinch myself to keep from saying, There, there. Like a lot of wives, she had learned that in the paper-scissors-rock game that goes on in most marriages, paper was a winner nine times out of ten.

"Well, Mr. Nader, will you help me?" I thought it over long enough to make a mental total of my checking-account balance.

"My rates are fifty dollars a day, plus expenses," I said, "and I'll need a hundred dollars in advance."

"I thought foundations paid your fees," she said, smiling.

"Not on private cases."

She gave me Larry Rendall's address, which was in the 8000 block on Whitehaven Parkway, and the address of the place where he worked three days a week, the El Ecolo in Georgetown, and a photo strip he had taken of himself in one of those bus station camera booths, and a nice pair of fifty dollar bills. I gave her a number she could reach me at in case anything came up, and a receipt.

After the sound of her heels died away, I opened a desk drawer and took out the can of V8 juice and bought myself a drink. Then I took a handful of vitamin C pills. Linus Pauling may be crazy, but no crazier than people who take those three-layer cold pills the size of a cookie that are nothing more than Micky Finn wearing a sandwich board.

I put on my hat and coat, turned out the light, and locked the inner office. I turned out the light in the outer office, but I left the door open so any clients who came looking for me while I was out could come in and read the back issues of *Consumer Reports* and sit on my Goodwill couches. They could also stretch out on a chaise longue and read *Photoplay* magazine and munch bonbons, but they'd have to have their own prop man for that.

When I got outside, there was a man sitting in a Chevelle and looking about as inconspicuous as a mouse in the bottom of a bottle of Coke. He'd need to be shaken, but I was in no hurry.

There aren't a lot of ways to get around Washington other than on foot if you don't own a car, which I don't, and if you have something against riding in them, which I do. You can ride a bicycle, but if you have enemies, it's like going deer-hunting with a Mafia triggerman. You can wait for the bus or you can wait for them to finish the subway sometime in 1978. As usual, I decided to take whichever one came first. The bus nosed out the subway, but it was a photo finish, and the motorman lodged a foul.

Following a Washington bus is about as easy as following the logic in a Nixon speech. They're much too slow for a car, and just a little too fast for the marrow-bone express. I waited until the man in the Chevelle got tired of slowing down and getting honked at and decided to take a turn around the block to give the bus a chance to get ahead, and then I got off, stood in a doorway until he went by again, and waited for the next bus. A lot of those little calendar pages had gone by the time it came.

The El Ecolo was on Prospect Street, next to George-town University. The E in El was a story high and lined in white lights that illuminated the rest of the lettering. It wasn't neon. Georgetown doesn't have any neon signs. Someone I knew a long time ago who lived in Georgetown told me what he liked about it was no neon and no Negroes. The way he said it, it sounded like he thought neon worked on Negroes the way those Koratron ultraviolet bug lures work on mosquitoes, and that if you didn't put up any neon signs, you didn't get any Negroes.

There used to be an El Morocco in Georgetown around the time I picked up the neon theory, and I was willing to bet this was the same place. Electric signs cost money. It probably had been the El Mocha in 1955, and someone who was now in marketing in Wilmington read a lot of poetry rhymed about as well as a laundry list, and when he was finished, people didn't clap, they snapped their fingers, because someone had been to Greenwich Village once, and in Greenwich Village they snap their fingers. And then it was the El Calypso, and then the El Twisto, and then the El Disco, and then the El Go-Go, and then maybe the El Olde English Pubbe, with beer in test tubes and a menu that offered mafhed potatoef and firloint fteak.

Right now it was a large brick room with Sierra Club posters on the wall and a picture of the earth as seen from the moon and a Navajo rug made by a tribe of navajos who moved to Rahway, New Jersey, and changed their name to Textel. There were about twenty tables and about as many people sitting at them and a bar along one wall. In a corner stood an old Seeberg jukebox that had probably sat, as tranquil as a buddha, spinning its little black prayer wheels through all the incarnations of the place. As I came in, a girl wearing one of those T-shirts that looked like it had been dyed with a stomach pump paid it a quarter, and it started chanting something you can hear for free downtown during rush hour.

I walked over to the bar. The bartender said, "Tara furba."

I didn't have a comeback.

"It's Ojibway for 'May your moccasins have wings.' The Ojibways were great poets. What'll it be?" I wondered how he'd like Wilmington.

There was a blackboard over the bar. I read it. "What's a Mandala?" I asked.

"Rum and mineral oil. You can get it with cider instead if you want. You see," he said seriously, "there has to be a balance between yin and yang or the stomach gets uptight."

"What's a Sutra?" I was getting desperate.

"Oh, that's a ham and swiss on banana bread, with

guacamole." I gave up and told him to bring me a glass of cider without the rum. The hell with the yang.

It came in an earthenware mug made by some Navajos who went to Osaka when their brothers went to New Jersey, and it cost 75 cents. I didn't mind because I knew part of the proceeds were going to buy scholarships for apple trees at forestry school.

"Hobba timagami," said the barkeep.

"Ojibway?"

"Right." He looked pleased. "It means 'May you never thirst more than the trout in the lake.'" I wasn't going to drink any, but I was afraid that might be an Ojibway way of telling him I thought his canoe was a lemon. It was Mott's, right out of the can, and the mug was dirty, and I was willing to bet there were cockroaches playing Simon Says in the guacamole, but I wasn't looking for health-code violations. I was looking for Larry Rendall. I said so.

"Larry? Sure, he works here. Or I think he does. He works Tuesdays, Thursdays, and Fridays, except he didn't come in last Friday, and he didn't call to tell anybody. The boss was pretty teed off. Why are you looking for him?"

"I want to ask him a few questions."

"He's not in any kind of trouble, is he? Say," he added brightly, "you're not a narc, are you?"

I said I wasn't.

"Larry's no head, I mean, he smokes a few joints once in a while, like anyone, but no hard stuff." I wondered what the Ojibway word for dumb fink was.

I showed him the picture strip just to make sure, and he said it was Larry, and I left him one of my cards and told him to have him call me if he came in. He said he wasn't sure he could remember all that, so I left him a dollar to buy a string to put around his finger with.

"Faruba toofla," he called as I left.

"Uckfay ooyay," I said.

Nobody did any translating.

It wasn't far to the address on Whitehaven, so I walked. It was eight o'clock, and Wisconsin Street was full of Christmas shoppers. In the Southeast, they were in Woolworth's buying little dolls that walked and talked and burst into flame and toy firetrucks with more sharp edges than a Swiss Army knife and modeling clay with poison enough to last the Borgias for a year, but in Georgetown they were in shops with names like The Committed Peacock and Perspicacity and Hemispherics, and they were buying sets of walnut blocks that illustrated the Pythagorean theorem and patchwork-quilt rag dolls made in Appalachia.

Number 8616 Whitehaven Parkway was part of a row of new, thin, two-story townhouses with built-in garages on a sloping street that ran along the edge of a little wooded strip they hadn't gotten around to blacktopping. It was still Georgetown, but the houses looked cheap, and it was almost as if the magic zoning spell that kept Georgetown colonial and graceful wasn't strong enough out here on the edges to keep out the first bits of aluminum siding and fake brick and stucco that the Wicked Witch has been using ever since candy prices got so high.

There weren't any lights on. I rang anyway for the benefit of any spectators, but there weren't any of those either, so I slipped the little plastic burglary tool one of the oil companies sent me in the mail between the door and the jamb and worked the bolt open. It had been intended to be employed for the kind of highway robbery oil companies indulge in, so I didn't feel like I was misusing it.

I closed the door and turned on the light. I took a step into the room, and then there was a flash behind my eyes, and the lights went out. When they came back on, Peter Pain was working on the back of my head with an air hammer, and I was on the floor and the door was open and someone was starting a car. I did an imitation of the mummy coming to life and chasing the professor who had ignored the curse of King Tut, but by the time I got to the street, the car was halfway down the hill. It was a late-model Buick Riviera with Virginia plates. I didn't get the number, but there were only three digits and some diagonal lettering, and in Virginia that's what they put on dealers' plates.

I went back inside and closed the door. This time I looked behind it, but no one was waiting in line to sap me. I walked through the living room to the kitchen and soaked a handful of paper towels in cold water and put them on the back of my head. This provides some mild transitory relief in minor cases of cranial trauma, or sapping, as it is sometimes called, and I recommend it for all my patients who are gumshoes.

I went back into the living room. It wasn't much to look at, and if you put up velvet ropes and charged $1 a head admission, you'd wind up at the end of the day $10 shy of a sawbuck. There were a few pieces of flotsam around that if you're a landlord you can put on your property and when people land there they have to pay double the rent. There were a few well-thumbed copies of *Road and Track* on a piece of furniture that got named Most Like a Desk in the little contest they had, and it had been rifled, but whoever did the rifling didn't come away with any Cellini miniatures.

I climbed the narrow flight of stairs that led to the upper floor. The bedroom was exactly what you'd expect to find if someone told you a family of kangaroos had just moved out.

I found Larry Rendall in the bathroom. He was sitting in the bathtub fully clothed in about an inch of red water, with his legs hanging over the rim. He'd had as many holes punched in him as that can of Zerex, but he'd had nine pints of Brand X in him instead of a quality antifreeze, and it had all leaked out. He looked like he had been dead for a couple of days, but I didn't feel like doing any sensitivity exercises with him, so I figured I might be off by twenty-four hours either way. It had been done with something thin and short, like a penknife, and it had probably been done by an amateur, since it had been done clumsily and too often. I guessed that the body had been put in the tub by someone who wasn't used to letting things spill on the floor.

I went into the bedroom and found some blood. I also found a gold tie clip with a GM logo on it, and on the back, engraved in script, "Salesman of the Year, 1970." That made me like the idea of the murder being done Friday night, since a tie clip lost Friday night might not be missed until Monday morning, and the person who missed it might not have a chance to come back looking for it until Monday night, just in time to sap a sleuth.

I wrapped the tie clip in my handkerchief and went downstairs. The door to the garage was in the kitchen. Mrs. Stallworth's Camaro was in the garage, and the keys were in it. I thought it over, then I opened the garage door, looked outside, drove the Camaro out, came back in, closed the garage door, and went back into the living room. I called the District Police and gave them the address and a reason for being interested in it and hung up. When I had done that, I turned out the light, closed the door, and got into the Camaro and drove it a few blocks away and parked it. Then I locked it and pocketed the keys, and headed up P Street with the light heart of a man who is leaving the scene of a murder, failing to report a directly related felony, and suppressing evidence.

It was eleven o'clock when I got back to the Excelsior Building. I guessed that it was named after the motto, and not the packing material, but the name told you it was a lousy building the same way a name like Majestic or Imperial tells you a hotel is a fleabag. Not all the windows were dark. When Congress is in session, the shyster lawyers, and the two-bit lobbyists, and the influence peddlers work late hours crawling all over bills, nibbling away at clauses, and leaving little amendments. When you wake up they're gone, but the water-pollution law doesn't prohibit liquid discharges anymore, and the acreage ownership limitation in Imperial Valley has picked up a couple of zeros, and a Congressman from Mississippi is getting $1 million for not growing rice on his tennis court.

I walked through the lobby with the marble lining that said Business the way Greek architecture says Government and Gothic arches say Religion. The night man was pushing a mop around, but no plastic Frisbee appeared to carry me over the floor, so I guessed he wasn't using the Acrowax. He took me up in the elevator and left me off at my floor. I went into my office and got the little pile of metal fragments Larry Rendall had been killed for out of the safe. Fifteen minutes and half a tube of Duco later, I had something that looked like an elongated bolt.

I got out the 1970 GM auto parts catalogue that sits in my library next to the *Bureau of Weights and Standards Reporter* and Volume 1 of *Decisions and Decrees of the Federal Trade Commission*. It took me until one o'clock to find it. It was Part GM 63CV8-20341-83995, but its friends called it Motor Mount Retaining Bolt. Four of them held the engine supporting frame to the underbody. And if their little hands got tired of holding the great big engine, it would drop onto the street. At 30 miles per hour, that would be a nuisance. At 60 miles per hour it would be positively annoying.

I had found four different models of Chevrolet V8, covering five years, that had the exact same bolt by the time I dozed off at around 4:00 A.M. I dreamed of driving very fast on a straight highway along which engines had been arranged in a slalom course. A voice sang, "Chevrolet—A Better Way to Go D.O.A.," and I kept trying to hit the brake, but there wasn't any. Rendall was sitting next me sticking bolts in all his holes and telling me not to worry, because he was already dead. Then parts started lazily flying out from under the hood and hitting the highway with a sound like clanging pails, and then the clanging turned into a ringing, and I woke up sweating. It was 8:30. The telephone was ringing. I answered it.

"Nader here," I said. I also said, "This phone is tapped." It was too early in the morning to think up any nifties.

"Mr. Nader, it's me." It was Mrs. Stallworth.

"Okay," I said. Most of the tiles in my tray were *q*'s and *x*'s so I wasn't going for any fancy triple-word scores.

"I just got a call from someone out on the Beltway who told me to meet him in an hour. It's about some letters I sent to someone I used to lend my car to that he's got. He thinks I have something he wants."

I was thinking about as quickly as one of those dinosaurs that had to send postcards to its feet to start walking. I waited for the little buzzer to tell me my time was up. "I guess I'll have to settle for the Speidel and the free shoes for life," I said.

"What?"

"Try it another way," I said.

She did some thinking. "Sounds like Olivetti," she said finally.

That worked. I was going to pay Spinetti a call anyway, but I didn't want her around. I had a feeling that the atmospheric lead-count was going to be unusually high. I told her to stay home.

"I can't," she said. "I've got to see to it I get those letters back."

I started to tell her that was what her $50-a-day was buying, but I was just spinning the V.U. meters on Mr. Hoover's Woolensaks. She had hung up. I dialed her number, but she had left the phone off the hook.

I washed my face. Then I went to the drawer where I

keep a spare shirt. It didn't say it had a ring around its collar, so I took off the soggy one I was wearing, and put it on.

I opened the drawer of my desk and took out the Triple-A Recommended Smith and Wesson .38 and strapped it on. Then I fitted my hat gently on my head. I caught a glimpse of myself in the mirror as I went out. I didn't look stronger than dirt.

Outside, nobody's clothes were turning white as I walked by.

Beltway Buick was in Falls Church, just past the intersection of Route 29 and the Beltway. Route 29 is the road the airport buses take out to Dulles, and for a couple of dollars the driver made an unscheduled stop before getting on I-495 and left me off under the overpass, about three hundred yards away from ten acres of cars with prices soaped in their windows and, overhead, a sign that said Beltway Buick and a lot of leathery red, white, and blue pennants strung up on wires and rattling in the wind and a big yellow board in the shape of a price tag with O.K. Used Cars on it. This told everyone that the odometers were as reliable as a sundial in a snowstorm.

I walked across the asphalt to the glass-walled building where they keep the Cars of the Decade for a year. I was looking at a Buick Riviera with dealer's plates parked out front, when a man wearing a suit made out of the stuff they used to use to jam radar came out and let me see his teeth.

"Any man who comes on foot must need a car bad," he sang. "Are you looking for something new, or can I show you one of our quality reconditioned cars?" There was a tone in his voice that said anyone who spent a lot of time walking probably wouldn't need a guidebook to find his way around the Kremlin.

"I'm looking for Spinetti," I said. He put his teeth away. Showing me Spinetti wasn't going to get him any bonuses.

"Right this way," he said, and led me through the showroom. The 1972 cars all had serious looks on their grilles. Last year they had foolish chromium grins. Times are bad all over.

"Didn't I read somewhere that Spinetti was Salesman of the Year in this region a year or so back?" I asked. That brought me a couple of incisors.

"You bet," he said. "Almost a thousand cars. It's an area record." He looked happier. Maybe I had let my Party membership expire.

Spinetti's office was in back, flanked by a pair of dusty rubber plants in tubs. His door had his name on it: Vincent J. Spinetti.

Mr. Happy Tooth did a quick shave-and-haircut on the door and warbled, "Mr. Spinetti, a gentleman to see you."

The door opened slowly. Our of habit I put my foot against it. What was making it open was a thick, heavy man in a conservative suit with a face that should have been served with horseradish and cocktail sauce and those little crackers. What was making it open slowly was fear. It was in his bulging eyes, and his pulpy face, and in the way his hand was testing the doorknob for resistance to vibration. He looked at me the way squirrels look at semis just before they get turned into little red lumps on the concrete.

"Yes," he croaked. If a city had his breath· they'd be taking some distilleries to court.

"The name is Nader," I said.

He kept looking. "Okay, Carter," he said. Carter went away.

We went into his office.

"Well, Mr. Nader, what can I do for you? He was trying to sound like Mr. Spinetti the Big-Shot Dealer. What he sounded like was little Vin Spinetti who got caught urinating on a neighbor's rosebush.

"On the road to Georgetown I met a man with seven stab wounds who found a defect in seven million Chevrolets. I got sapped once. Now here's the poser: How many numbers do I have to dial to get the District Police?" I reached for his phone.

"I don't know what you're talking about," he said. That act held up for the time it took me to dial one number.

He hit the cradle button with a pudgy finger. "Who are you and what do you want?"

I showed him a card.

"Public eye, huh?" He made it sound like something you took drops for.

"I'm not the Man from Glad."

"Who are you working for?"

"I've got seven million and one clients. The first seven million want to know about a car they own that gets a kick out of dropping its load in the road. The last one wants some letters back. Since she's footing the bill, let's talk about her first."

"Letters?" He was getting confident. I wasn't the law. Maybe if he zipped up his fly very quick, his mommy would never know.

"No more games, Spinetti," I said. "Let me tell you the way I see it, and if I leave anything out, you tell me afterwards. Sometime last week Larry Rendall drove out here in a Camaro you sold to a Mrs. Stallworth and told you he had something the boys in Detroit would pay a lot to keep from getting around. He probably picked you because he figured it didn't much matter who in GM he went to, because word would get back. He gave you the name of a part and a stock number, and told you what happened to it when you hit it with a hammer, and said to get in touch with him when you had some word. It didn't mean anything to you, but you figured it wouldn't look good on your record if there was something in what he was saying and you let it go by, so you make a call, and they tell you they'll look into it. Pretty soon they call back, and they tell you to stall him, deal with him, anything, until they can get some people out from Detroit to see him, and they talk to you about stock options and bonuses if it all goes all right." Spinetti had a silly smile on his face. He wasn't looking at me. He was smelling the roses and looking at the glistening leaves. "So you called Rendall and arranged to meet him at his place Friday night. When you got there, Rendall was cocky and named some ridiculous sum, and laughed at you, and maybe you got mad or maybe you figured a dead Larry Rendall would please the company even more than a bought-off one, maybe ten thousand shares more, who knows? So you did a little stabbing, and Rendall did a lot of struggling and took a tie clip off you, but you were in a hurry and afraid and didn't notice. You found it missing Monday morning, so you went back Monday night, and searched for it, but all you found were some love letters. You figured they might buy you some silence from Mrs. Stallworth if Larry had done any talking to her, and that might come in handy, because by now the boys from Detroit are all over the place, and they don't like the way you've been handling things, and they tell you Mrs. Stallworth has gone to see a dick. But just as you're about to leave, some gumshoe comes up and plays with the doorbell, and then with the lock, and you give him a sap to eat. But what do you know? He gets your license number,"— this was for drama—""and finds a tie clip."

The first time I said those words Spinetti had jerked like those dummies in the collision tests. He did the second time, too.

"What do you want me to do?" It was a whimper.

"First of all, you're going to give me the letters." Mrs. Stallworth had a good ear for an entrance line, because right then Carter did his little paradiddle on the door, and she walked in. As soon as Carter closed it, she brought out a little nickle-plated .22 of the kind women keep in their purses so muggers will have something to shoot them with in case they forget to bring their own.

"I want those letters," she said. The gun didn't say anything, but it looked like it was getting ready to.

"Put it away, Mrs. Stallworth," I said. "Mr. Spinetti was just about to give them to me, weren't you, Mr. Spinetti?" He was. One of the fat little crabs that lived on the ends of his wrists scuttled into a drawer and came out with a sheaf of letters. Penny snatched them, took a quick look, and then stuffed them in her purse.

"No Xeroxes?" I said. He shook his head no. His hand was heading back into the drawer, so I picked up a heavy brass ruler he had on his desk that had the Golden Rule printed on it, and hit it. Then I went over and took the gun it had been looking for out of the drawer and put it in my pocket.

Spinetti looked at his hand. I had rapped his knuckles, and maybe that was the end of it.

I told Penny to put away the gun again, and this time she did. Then I had a bright idea and told her to go home, but I was a little late. The door opened without a knock and a half-dozen hard-looking men in gray suits came in. They were on the company payroll, but I was willing to bet they weren't the Pontiac Choirboys.

Spinetti's face did an impression of the underbelly of a grouper.

One of the men said, "Let's go," and just in case Spinetti hadn't heard this, two more picked him up out of his chair and took him out. Spinetti had made a mess. Messes were bad for business. They were tidying up. In about an hour he was going to be one more body by Fisher.

The man who seemed to be giving the orders looked at me. "Don't I know you?" he said.

I took a chance. Maybe this was a different set of goons from the ones that had been tailing me and calling in death threats. Maybe it was a special set who took care of this kind of work.

"No, sir," I said, trying to sound as gee-whiz as I could. "The wife and I were just in looking at a Le Mans. Say, are you G-men?" I figured I'd make it as easy for him as I could.

He reached in his pocket. I had a feeling he wasn't going to show me his Lark pack. He took out a gun. He used it as a badge to fool Mr. and Mrs. Booby.

"That's right, folks," he said. "And you'll be doing the government a big favor if you keep quiet about this."

"Gosh," I said, "you bet. We won't say a thing, will we, Velma?"

"No siree," said Velma. "We won't breathe a word." She was good. Paper covers rock.

They went out.

We sat still for five minutes. Then I got up. Someone had replaced my legs with a pair of swizzle sticks.

"Now what?" said Penny Stallworth.

"Now you go home. Here are the keys to your car. It was in Rendall's garage. It's parked on Wisconsin, near P Street. Don't get it for a couple of days. Rendall's dead. Spinetti killed him. I haven't done any talking to the law, and it doesn't look like I'm going to have to now, but if I do have to, there's no way I can tell it and leave you out of it."

She didn't bother to look sad. She took the keys and put them in her purse and took out some bills.

"Nix," I said. "You gave me $100. I worked two days. We're quits."

She put the money away, and then she gave me the kind of kiss uncles get, and then she walked away very fast.

I gave her a few minutes and then I walked outside. Carter was talking to a couple of suckers who weren't a shamus and his client pretending to be rubes. He didn't see me go.

I walked along the highway to a place where I could flag the bus. The people going by in their cars made sighing noises, and whether it was the people who made them, or the cars, you couldn't tell. Defective people in defective cars, moving fast, but not fast enough. It didn't matter whether you ended up sitting in a bathtub with too many holes in your body to repair, or whether you did something stupid and they came and took you away...it was all the same. Everyone goes back, sooner or later, back in the big recall.

When I got back downtown I made some telephone calls to a few Congressmen and sent the bolt with some notes to a man I know in the National Traffic Safety Bureau. After that I went home.

National Lampoon. *This Side of Parodies*. NY: Warner Books, 1974.

Christopher Ward

The Pink Murder Case

The 1920s were fertile times for humor in the United States. *Life* was then a humor magazine, as were *Judge* and *College Humor*. Periodicals as unlikely as the *Detroit Athletic Club News* and *The Yale Review* regularly printed Benchley and Ford. Every major city had half a dozen or more competing newspapers, hard as it is to believe today, with most of them having literary supplements, hard as that is to believe, and humorists could be found even there, amazing as *that* is to believe in these overly serious times.

In the early part of the decade, the *Literary Review of the New York Evening Post* began publishing Christopher Ward's parodies. He produced sufficient to eventually fill two collections, *The Triumph of the Nut* and *Twisted Tales*, before the inevitable attack of seriousness (check out Ford and Wallach) induced him to abandon humor for a series of heavyweight and well-received tomes on America's colonial and revolutionary war periods.

Ward had mostly stopped writing parodies in 1929 when this piece appeared, but the Philo Vance craze proved too much to resist. To those not around at the time, it's difficult to convey how Vance-wild readers became for those few years. The closest analogy would be the way the world went Bond-crazy after the first movies came out in the early 1960s. Foppish, dilettantish, dropping obscure allusions to Coptic poetry as readily as he dropped the g's from the endings of his words, Vance was as unlikely a hero as his highbrow inventor, Willard Huntington Wright (under the pen name of S. S. Van Dine), was a mystery writer.

Composed almost entirely of eccentricities, Vance was hated by other writers in proportion about equal to the public's love. Parodies surfaced almost immediately. Ogden Nash coupleted, "Philo Vance/Needs a kick in the pance," and Corey Ford pummeled Vance in his parody collection, "The John Riddell Murder Case." (All of Vance's offerings were "Murder Case"s.) Ward's parody is particularly unmerciful, and not to be missed by connoisseurs of venom.

*   *   *

By S. S. Veendan

Author of the "Green," "Canary," Mauve," and "Beige Murder Cases"

CHAPTER I

THE HOUSE ON THE MARSH

(Tuesday, February 22, 1732; 1 A.M.)

AMONG ALL the vari-colored murder cases from which Philo Pants has derived his reputation and I my income during the last few years, certainly there was none more horrifying, nor, in its outcome, more astounding than the Pink one.

My friend Pants was, as I have often written, a young social aristocrat with carefully chiselled features, especially a fine, hand-engraved, aquamarine nose. His conversation was the most completely satisfying I have ever known. No one ever felt the need of a second dose.

He was a close friend of Barker,* the District Attorney, who entrusted to him the most interesting murder cases, much to my profit, since thus the murderer was given time to kill a whole book-full of people,† which is really necessary nowadays to keep the reader's interest. So it was that the frightful Pink holocaust was made possible. Pants had been for several days immersed in a Coptic translation of Schizzenheimer's "Nuovi Studi de la Physiologie des Heisshundes." He could not read Coptic, but was trying to decide which was the right side up of the fascinating volume, when Barker came in.

"A new murder for you, Pants," said Barker gloomily.

"Oh, I say, don't y' know, eh what?" drawled Pants. "How dashed amusin'. Most intriguin' and all that sort of thing. I could bear to hear about the bally homicide, old bean, don't y' know."

Barker frowned, glowered, and gritted his teeth. Pants's parts of speech always had this effect on him.

"It's a Pink case this time," he grumbled. "They're bad enough plain, but when they come in colors they're devilish. Some day a Scotch plaid will turn up and finish me."

"Who's the jolly old victim of the distressin' crime? My flutterin' heart's anguished to know."

---

*George A. ("Gabby") Barker was the most efficient District Attorney of that name New York ever had. After retirement from office, he became a private citizen.

† The Blue Murder Case (Scribblers, 1929; $2.50).

The Cardinal Murder Case (Scribblers, 1927; $2.50).

Barker tore his hair and spat through his teeth grudgingly. "Alonzo Pink," he said, with biting sarcasm.

"I say, y' know, you don't say so," drawled Pants. "Old pal of mine. Spent last evenin' with him, discussin' terra cotta ornamentation of renaissance patisseries and all that. Dead, eh? Amusin' predicament, eh what?"

"Know any other Pinks?" asked Barker in a rage.

"Whole dashed lot, Citronella and Palooka, sisters, Hercules, brother, contemp'ry offspring on heredit-ry sire, old Paresis Pink, bally old blighter."

"Come along, then," gargled Barker furiously.

CHAPTER II

SHRIEKS IN THE NIGHT

(Tuesday, December 25, 1929; 3 A.M.)

The Pink mansion stood on Broadway three blocks south of the Battery, a gloomy pile, embowered in funeral yews and gaunt weeping willows. A foreboding of woe came over me as we neared its ghastly portal.

Snoot, the butler, admitted us. A man of more sinister aspect I have never seen. He had but one eye on each side of his nose and his mouth was practically horizontal. In a sepulchral voice, he told us he had found Alonzo dead in his bedroom, shot through the head, and that all the doors and windows were locked on the inside. A Colt .32 lay by his side. Then he took us to the chamber of death.

"Oh, I say, my word!" drawled Pants. "How dashed amusin'!"

"What?" barked Barker.

"Don't notice anything funny, eh? Of course, you wouldn't. Why, man, the jolly old corpse is standin' on its head."

And so it was, but only the quick eye of Philo Pants had marked the fact.

"Now," drawled Pants, "we'll interview the caressin' family."

Citronella Pink met us in the library. She was gently but firmly dressed in a jade green bathing suit, a brown bowler, and white spats. She was a beautiful woman, but something about her made me think of either Lucrezia Borgia or Lizzie Borden or both.

"Ever do any shootin', Citronella?" drawled Pants.

"Lots," she said nonchalantly, whipping out a Colt .32.

"Ever shoot Alonzo?"

"Don't you wish you knew?" she said teasingly. "Ask Herc, he knows."

We found Hercules and his sister, Palooka, in the garage. They were shooting at each other with .32 Colts, but, as he had a harelip and St. Vitus's dance and she was cockeyed, neither had hit the other. Pants turned to Barker.

"Think I'll take on this amusin' pair after dinner," he drawled. "Give the servants jolly old once over now."

The entire staff was paraded for inspection. They all looked like jailbirds, and it was, indeed, found that they all were. Suspicion having thus been satisfactorily distributed, Pants dismissed Barker. "Run along, old fruit," he drawled. "I'll carry on with silly old Veendam."

CHAPTER III

GHOULS AND VAMPIRES

(Thursday, April 1, 1066; 4 A.M.)

At 9:30 the next morning Pants, in purple velvet pajamas, was sipping his cognac as he idly turned the leaves of an illuminated copy of Teufelsdrockh's "Ichweissnicht

Wassolles Bedeutendass Ichsotraurigbin," when our phone rang.

"Barker speaking," said an agitated voice. "Pink case again. Palooka and Hercules found dead in rooms. Doors and windows all locked inside. Colt .32 by side each. Come at once. Mother."

"How deuced annoyin'," drawled Pants. "Must go around to jolly old slaughter-house again."

We met Barker there. "Undoubtedly an inside job," said he, "though it probably started outside. Ku-Klux, I think, with a dash of Mafia and a sprinkling of Paprika. By their fingerprints I've identified Snoot as the late Belle Boyd, the Beautiful Rebel Spy, and the parlor maid as Jesse James."

Pants looked at him with pained surprise. "Listen, Barker," he said earnestly. "There's something terrible going on here. Can't you feel it? In this lonely old mansion—poor thing!—polluted with a miasma of corrupt and rotting ambitions, black hatreds, hideous impulses, rheumatism, catarrh, coughs, colds, and indigestion—in this loathly mansion three bozos have been bumped off. Deuced amusin', eh what? Must have little old parley-voo with Citronella. Roll along, old egg. Toodle-oo and all that sort of thing."

Gasping with rage, Barker left Philo Pants, the mastermind, to pursue his inquiries.

CHAPTER IV

RED DARRELL'S REVENGE

(St. Valentine's Day, 1444, 5 A.M.)

At 9:30 the following morning Barker again appeared at

our apartment. He was accompanied by Detective Bogan*
and two policemen. Pants greeted the party with his usual
charming insouciance.

"Ah, bobbies, what? Why the parade?"

"New development in the Pink case," said Barker in a
tone of forbearance. "Citronella dead as per former plans
and specifications."

"Pinks all wiped out, eh?" drawled Pants brightly· "No
more cannon-fodder, crime wave will subside."

"Wait a bit," hissed Barker. "I've been studying this case
and I've reached certain conclusions. First, these victims
were all found dead in locked rooms, shot through heads
with .32 calibre bullets and—mark this hitherto dis-
regarded fact—a .32 Colt was found by the side of each!
Do you see what that means? I didn't until Bogan told me.
It was in each and every case—*suicide.*" His voice sunk to a
whisper as he pronounced the unexpected and dreadful
word.

"Very well," he went on. " 'Why?' I asked Bogan. He
answered like a flash—'Bughouse.' A logical working
hypothesis, I said to myself. 'Why bughouse?' I asked
Bogan. He answered in two words. But before I tell you
what they were let me ask you a few questions. Who was
with Alonzo Pink the evening before he shot himself? Who
questioned Hercules and Palooka the day before their fatal
night? Who 'parley-vooed' with Citronella before she shuffled off? The answer is in the two words of the astute
Bogan—*Philo Pants!*

"It was you, Pants. Your blithering blah, your musical-
comedy English accent drove these people mad, made

---

*Thomas Aquinas Bogan was first on the scene of the murders of Elwell and
Arnold Rothstein and in the Dorothy Arnold disappearance case. He is now
raising turtle-doves in Hoboken.

them fly for relief to self-destruction. You are their murderer. And you, Veendam, were not only his wretched accomplice in this case, but your books, disseminating his words, have sowed the seeds of madness in many homes. Arrest these men!"

As the cops stepped forward, Philo Pants lightly laughed and, unscrewing the tip of his aquamarine nose, took from a cavity within two pellets.

"Catch, old dear," he drawled, as he tossed one to me. "Sorry to disappoint, old fruit," he said to Barker. "It's dashed distressin', but must say toodle-oo and all that sort of thing."

Then together we swallowed the pellets and in a moment we both lay dead upon the floor.

"As usual," said Barker resignedly, "cyanide of potassium."

The Art of the Mystery Story. Ed. by Howard Haycraft. NY: Simon & Schuster, 1946.

James Thurber

The White Rabbit Caper

All his life James Thurber wrote about three separate but weirdly equal species: men, women, and animals. In "The Secret Life of Walter Mitty" and other stories Thurber polished the "little man" formula to a high gloss. Those "frustrated, fugitive beings" (as E. B. White called them) were sweetly buffeted by life, always caught by powerful forces they didn't understand. Thurber's women—strong, willful, and always bigger than their menfolk—were usually the major force involved.

Somehow Thurber's animals rounded out the equation. Think of his first and still most famous cartoon in which a seal pokes over the headboard of a Thurber couple's bed as the wife snarls, "All right, have it your way—you heard a seal bark."

Thurber's stories and drawings were childlike only on the surface. Underneath they packed a mighty punch. Despite his trepidations—"One of the greatest fears of the humorous writer is that he has spent three weeks writing

105

something done faster and better by Benchley in 1919" (but
see who Benchley gives the credit to)—his stories remained
uniquely his own, as did his art. A better draftsman once
collared *New Yorker* editor Harold Ross to ask, "Why do you
reject drawings of mine and print stuff by that fifth-rate
artist Thurber?" Ross gave as spirited a defense as was
possible. "Third rate," he said.

Thurber's books were as filled with his animal drawings
as animals abounded in the tall tales of his boyhood in
Columbus, his collection of modern fables, and the *New
Yorker* pieces he called casuals. Typical Thurber titles
include *The Owl in the Attic, The Seal in the Bedroom, Thurber's
Dogs, The Beast in Me and Other Animals.* His one major play
is even called *The Male Animal.*

And it is to animals he turned when he wanted to parody
the increasingly violent detective yarns being featured on
radio mystery programs and in the paperback pulps in the
early 1950s, Mickey Spillane's era. Picture for yourself
Thurber's own cartoon animals playing the parts in this
hardboiled bedtime story for very tough children.

* * *

(AS THE BOYS WHO TURN OUT THE MYSTERY PROGRAMS
ON THE AIR MIGHT WRITE A STORY FOR CHILDREN)

FRED FOX was pouring himself a slug of rye when the door
of his office opened and in hopped old Mrs. Rabbit. She
was a white rabbit with pink eyes, and she wore a shawl on
her head, and gold-rimmed spectacles.

"I want you to find Daphne," she said tearfully, and she
handed Fred Fox a snapshot of a white rabbit with pink
eyes that looked to him like a picture of every other white
rabbit with pink eyes.

"When did she hop the hutch?" asked Fred Fox.

"Yesterday," said old Mrs. Rabbit. "She is only eighteen

months old, and I am afraid that some superstitious creature has killed her for one of her feet."

Fred Fox turned the snapshot over and put it in his pocket. "Has this bunny got a throb?" he asked.

"Yes," said old Mrs. Rabbit. "Franz Frog, repulsive owner of the notorious Lily Pad Night Club."

Fred Fox leaped to his feet. "Come on, Grandma," he said, "and don't step on your ears. We got to move fast."

On the way to the Lily Pad Night Club, old Mrs. Rabbit scampered so fast that Fred Fox had all he could do to keep up with her. "Daphne is my great-great-great-great-great-granddaughter, if my memory serves," said old Mrs. Rabbit. "I have thirty-nine thousand descendants."

"This isn't going to be easy," said Fred Fox. "Maybe you should have gone to a magician with a hat."

"But she is the only one named Daphne," said old Mrs. Rabbit, "and she lived alone with me on my great carrot farm."

They came to a broad brook. "Skip it!" said Fred Fox.

"Keep a civil tongue in your head, young man," snapped old Mrs. Rabbit.

Just as they got to the Lily Pad, a dandelion clock struck twelve noon. Fred Fox pushed the button on the great green door, on which was painted a white water lily. The door opened an eighth of an inch, and Ben Rat peered out. "Beat it," he said, but Fred Fox shoved the door open, and old Mrs. Rabbit followed him into a cool green hallway, softly but restlessly lighted by thousands of fireflies imprisoned in the hollow crystal pendants of an enormous chandelier. At the right there was a flight of green-carpeted stairs, and at the bottom of the steps the door to the cloakroom. Straight ahead, at the end of the long hallway, was the cool green door to Franz Frog's office.

"Beat it," said Ben Rat again.

"Talk nice," said Fred Fox, "or I'll seal your house up with tin. Where's the Croaker?"

"Once a gumpaw, always a gumpaw," grumbled Ben Rat. "He's in his office."

"With Daphne?"

"Who's Daphne?" asked Ben Rat.

"My great-great-great-great-great-granddaughter," said old Mrs. Rabbit.

"Nobody's that great," snarled Ben Rat.

FRED FOX opened the cool green door and went into Franz Frog's office, followed by old Mrs. Rabbit and Ben Rat. The owner of the Lily Pad sat behind his desk, wearing a green suit, green shirt, green tie, green socks, and green shoes. He had an emerald tie pin and seven emerald rings. "Whong yo wong, Fonnxx?" he rumbled in a cold, green, cavernous voice. His eyes bulged and his throat began to swell ominously.

"He's going to croak," explained Ben Rat.

"Nuts," said Fred Fox. "He'll outlive all of us."

"Glunk," croaked Franz Frog.

Ben Rat glared at Fred Fox. "You oughta go on the stage," he snarled.

"Where's Daphne?" demanded Fred Fox.

"Hoong Dangneng?" asked Franz Frog.

"Your bunny friend," said Fred Fox.

"Nawng," said Franz Frog.

Fred Fox picked up a cello in a corner and put it down. It was too light to contain a rabbit. The front-door bell rang. "I'll get it," said Fred Fox. It was Oliver (Hoot) Owl, a notorious fly-by-night. "What're you doing up at this hour, Hoot?" asked Fred Fox.

"I'm trying to blind myself, so I'll confess," said Hoot Owl testily.

"Confess to what?" snapped Fred Fox.

"What can't you solve?" asked Hoot Owl.

"The disappearance of Daphne," said Fred Fox.

"Who's Daphne?" asked Hoot Owl.

Franz Frog hopped out of his office into the hall. Ben Rat and old Mrs. Rabbit followed him.

Down the steps from the second floor came Sherman Stork, carrying a white muffler or something and grinning foolishly.

"Well, bless my soul!" said Fred Fox. "If it isn't old mid-husband himself! What did you do with Daphne?"

"Who's Daphne?" asked Sherman Stork.

"Fox thinks somebody killed Daphne Rabbit," said Ben Rat.

"Fonnxx cung brong," rumbled Franz Frog.

"I *could* be wrong," said Fred Fox, "but I'm not." He pulled open the cloakroom door at the bottom of the steps, and the dead body of a female white rabbit toppled furrily onto the cool green carpet. Her head had been bashed in by a heavy blunt instrument.

"Daphne!" screamed old Mrs. Rabbit, bursting into tears.

"I can't see a thing," said Hoot Owl.

"It's a dead white rabbit," said Ben Rat. "Anybody can see that. You're dumb."

"I'm wise!" said Hoot Owl indignantly. "I know everything."

"Jeeng Crine," moaned Franz Frog. He stared up at the chandelier, his eyes bulging and his mammoth mouth gaping open. All the fireflies were frightened and went out.

The cool green hallway became pitch dark. There was a shriek in the black, and a feathery "plump." The fireflies lighted up to see what had happened. Hoot Owl lay dead on the cool green carpet, his head bashed in by a heavy blunt instrument. Ben Rat, Franz Frog, Sherman Stork, old Mrs. Rabbit, and Fred Fox stared at Hoot Owl. Over the cool green carpet crawled a warm red stain, whose source was the body of Hoot Owl. He lay like a feather duster.

"Murder!" squealed old Mrs. Rabbit.

"Nobody leaves this hallway!" snapped Fred Fox. "There's a killer loose in this club!"

"I am not used to death," said Sherman Stork.

"Roong!" groaned Franz Frog.

"He says he's ruined," said Ben Rat, but Fred Fox wasn't listening. He was looking for a heavy blunt instrument. There wasn't any.

"Search them!" cried old Mrs. Rabbit. "Somebody has a sap, or a sock full of sand, or something!"

"Yeh," said Fred Fox. "Ben Rat is a sap—maybe someone swung him by his tail."

"You oughta go on the stage," snarled Ben Rat.

FRED FOX searched the suspects, but he found no concealed weapon. "You could have strangled them with that muffler," Fred Fox told Sherman Stork.

"But they were not strangled," said Sherman Stork.

Fred Fox turned to Ben Rat. "You could have bitten them to death with your ugly teeth," he said.

"But they weren't bitten to death, said Ben Rat.

Fred Fox stared at Franz Frog. "You could have scared them to death with your ugly face," he said.

"Bung wung screng ta deng," said Franz Frog.

"You're right," admitted Fred Fox."They weren't. Where's old Mrs. Rabbit?" he asked suddenly.

"I'm hiding in here," called old Mrs. Rabbit from the cloakroom. "I'm frightened."

Fred Fox got her out of the cool green sanctuary and went in himself. It was dark. He groped around on the cool green carpet. He didn't know what he was looking for, but he found it, a small object lying in a far corner. He put it in his pocket and came out of the cloakroom.

"What'd you find, shamus?" asked Ben Rat apprehensively.

"Exhibit A," said Fred Fox casually.

"Sahng plang keeng," Moaned Franz Frog.

"He says somebody's playing for keeps," said Ben Rat.

"He can say that again," said Fred Fox as the front door was flung open and Inspector Mastiff trotted in, followed by Sergeant Dachshund.

"Well, well, look who's muzzling in," said Fred Fox.

"What have we got here?" barked Inspector Mastiff.

"I hate a private nose," said Sergeant Dachshund.

Fred Fox grinned at him. "What happened to your legs from the knees down, sport?" he asked.

"Drop dead," snarled Sergeant Dachsund.

"Quiet, both of you!" snapped Inspector Mastiff. "I know Ollie Owl, but who's the twenty-dollar Easter present from Schrafft's?" He turned on Fred Fox. "If this bunny's head comes off and she's filled with candy, I'll have your badge, Fox," he growled.

"She's real, Inspector," said Fred Fox. "Real dead, too. How did you pick up the scent?"

Inspector Mastiff howled. "The Sergeant thought he smelled a rat at the Lily club," he said. "Wrong again, as usual. Who's this dead rabbit?"

"She's my great-great-great-great-great granddaughter," sobbed old Mrs. Rabbit.

Fred Fox lighted a cigarette. "Oh, no, she isn't, sweetheart," he said coolly, "You are *her* great-great-great-great-great granddaughter." Pink lightning flared in the live white rabbit's eyes. "You killed the old lady, so you could take over her carrot farm," continued Fred Fox, "and then you killed Hoot Owl."

"I'll Kill you, too, shamus!" shrieked Daphne Rabbit.

"Put the cuffs on her, Sergeant," barked Inspector Mastiff. Sergeant Dachsund put a pair of handcuffs on the front legs of the dead rabbit. "Not *her,* you dumb kraut!"

yelped Inspector Mastiff. It was too late. Daphne Rabbit had jumped through a windowpane and run away, with the Sergeant in hot pursuit.

"ALL WHITE RABBITS look alike to me," growled Inspector Mastiff. "How could you tell them apart—from their ears?"

"No," said Fred Fox. "From their years. The white rabbit that called on me darn near beat me to the Lily Pad, and no old woman can do that."

"Don't brag," said Inspector Mastiff. "Spryness isn't enough. What else?"

"She understood expressions an old rabbit doesn't know," said Fred Fox, "like 'hop the hutch' and 'throb' and 'skip it' and 'sap.'"

"You can't hang a rabbit for her vocabulary," said Inspector Mastiff. "Come again."

Fred Fox pulled the snapshot out of his pocket. "The white rabbit who called on me told me Daphne was eighteen months old," he said, "but read what it says on the back of this picture."

Inspector Mastiff took the snapshot, turned it over and read," "Daphne on her second birthday.'"

"Yes," said Fred Fox. "Daphne knocked six months off her age. You see, Inspector, she couldn't read the writing on the snapshot, because those weren't her spectacles she was wearing."

"Now wait a minute," growled Inspector Mastiff. "Why did she kill Hoot Owl?"

"Elementary, my dear Mastiff," said Fred Fox. "Hoot Owl lived in an oak tree, and she was afraid he saw her burrowing into the club last night, dragging Grandma. She heard Hoot Owl say, 'I'm wise. I know everything,' and so she killed him."

"What with?" demanded the Inspector.

"Her right hind foot," said Fred Fox. "I was looking for a concealed weapon, and all the time she was carrying her heavy blunt instrument openly."

"Well, what do you know!" exclaimed Inspector Mastiff. "Do you think Hoot Owl really saw her?"

"Could be," said Fred Fox. "I happen to think he was bragging about his wisdom in general and not about a particular piece of information, but your guess is as good as mine."

"What did you pick up in the cloakroom?" squeaked Ben Rat.

"The final strand in the rope that will hang Daphne," said Fred Fox. "I knew she didn't go in there to hide. She went in there to look for something she lost last night. If she'd been frightened, she would have hidden when the flies went out, but she went in there after the flies lighted up again."

"That adds up," said Inspector Mastiff grudgingly. "What was it she was looking for?"

"Well," said Fred Fox, "she heard something drop in the dark when she dragged Grandma in there last night and she thought it was a button, or a buckle, or a bead, or a bangle, or a brooch that would incriminate her. That's why she rang me in on the case. She couldn't come here alone to look for it."

"Well, what was it, Fox?" snapped Inspector Mastiff.

"A carrot," said Fred Fox, and he took it out of his pocket, "probably fell out of old Mrs. Rabbit's reticule, if you like irony."

"One more question," said Inspector Mastiff. "Why plant the body in the Lily Pad?"

"Easy," said Fred Fox. "She wanted to throw suspicion on the Croaker, a well-known lady-killer."

"Nawng," rumbled Franz Frog.

"Well, there it is, Inspector," said Fred Fox, "all wrapped up for you and tied with ribbons."

Ben Rat disappeared into a wall. Franz Frog hopped back to his office.

"Mercy!" cried Sherman Stork. "I'm late for an appointment!" He flew to the front door and opened it.

There stood Daphne Rabbit, holding the unconscious form of Sergeant Dachshund. "I give up," she said. "I surrender."

"Is he dead?" asked Inspector Mastiff hopefully.

"No," said Daphne Rabbit. "He fainted."

"I never have any luck," growled Inspector Mastiff.

Fred Fox leaned over and pointed to Daphne's right hind foot. "Owl feathers," he said. "She's all yours, Inspector."

"Thanks, Fox," said Inspector Mastiff. "I'll throw something your way someday."

"Make it a nice, plump Plymouth Rock pullet," said Fred Fox, and he sauntered out of the Lily Pad.

BACK IN HIS OFFICE, Fred Fox dictated his report on the White Rabbit Caper to his secretary, Lura Fox. "Period. End of report," he said finally, toying with the emerald stickpin he had taken from Franz Frog's green necktie when the fireflies went out.

"Is she pretty?" asked Lura Fox.

"Daphne? Quite a dish," said Fred Fox, "but I like my rabbits stewed, and I'm afraid little Daphne is going to fry."

"But she's so young, Fred!" cried Lura Fox. "Only eighteen months!"

"You weren't listening," said Fred Fox.

"How did you know she wasn't interested in Franz Frog?" asked Lura Fox.

"Simple," said Fred Fox. "Wrong species."

"What became of the candy, Fred?" asked Lura Fox.
Fred Fox stared at her. "What candy?" he asked blankly.
Lura Fox suddenly burst into tears. "She was so soft, and warm, and cuddly, Fred," she wailed.

Fred Fox filled a glass with rye, drank it slowly, set down the glass, and sighed grimly. "Sour racket," he said.

James Thurber. *Thurber Country.* NY: Simon & Schuster/Touchstone, 1981.

Garrison Keillor

Jack Schmidt, Arts Administrator

Here's some news that may surprise a few people. By the time you first heard *A Prairie Home Companion* when it went national in 1980, Garrison Keillor had already had a long and inventive career as a *New Yorker* writer. In fact, his collection of short pieces, *Happy to Be Here,* appeared in 1981 and, like few other first books of short stories, rose up the best seller lists.

Great parody requires an almost perfect ear for language, and if any organ other than that magnificent ideal-for-radio baritone voice of his propelled Keillor to fame, it was his ear. Keillor's writing precisely catches distinctive rhythms and phrases, and lays bare his concerns about language on almost every page. Those who only know the characters from Lake Wobegon might be taken aback at some of his other targets. Who else has parodied Richard Brautigan?

Private eye parodies are all about language: the extremely imitable patter between the shamus and the lowlifes around him, the metaphors that stop readers dead in their tracks. An ex-hotel dick, Keillor's Jack Schmidt is a paperback fantasy brought to respectability. Keillor's titles for those paperbacks (in addition to ones you'll see below, they include *Murder from Room Service, The Magic Fingers Gang, Dead Man: Do Not Disturb,* and *Mr. Chatsworth Checks Out*) perfectly capture the pulp paperback era that will forever be our image of the eye. Jack Schmidt may have left the rough and tumble street life for the bureaucratic precincts of administration but I think you'll find that the patter is only funnier for falling between the lines of a plot about—arts funding.

* * *

IT WAS ONE OF THOSE SWELTERING DAYS toward the end of the fiscal year when Minneapolis smells of melting asphalt and foundation money is as tight as a rusted nut. Ninety-six, the radio said on the way in from the airport, and back at my office in the Acme Building I was trying to fan the memory of ocean breezes in Hawaii, where I had just spent two days attending a conference on midwestern regionalism.

It wasn't working. I was sitting down, jacket off, feet up, looking at the business end of an air conditioner, and a numb spot was forming around my left ear to which I was holding a telephone and listening to Bobby Jo, my secretary at the Twin Cities Arts Mall, four blocks away, reading little red numerals off a sheet of paper. We had only two days before the books snapped shut, and our administrative budget had sprung a deficit big enough to drive a car through—a car full of accountants. I could feel a dark sweat stain spreading across the back of my best blue shirt.

"Listen," I sputtered, "I still got some loose bucks in the publicity budget. Let's transfer that to administration."

"J.S.," she sighed, "I just got done telling you. Those loose bucks are as spent as an octogenarian after an all-night bender. Right now we're using more red ink than the funny papers, and yesterday we bounced three checks right off the bottom of the account. That budget is so unbalanced, it's liable to go out and shoot somebody."

You could've knocked me over with a rock.

"Sweetheart," I lied quietly, hoping she couldn't hear my heavy breathing, "don't worry about it. Old Jack has been around the block once or twice. I'll straighten it out."

"Payday is tomorrow," she sniffed sharply. "Twelve noon."

The Arts Mall is just one of thirty-seven arts organizations I administer, a chain that stretches from the Anaheim Puppet Theatre to the Title IX Poetry Center in Bangor, and I could have let it go down the tubes, but hell, I kind of like the joint. It's an old Henny Penny supermarket that we renovated in 1976 when Bicentennial money was wandering around like helpless buffalo, and it houses seventeen little shops—mainly pottery and macrame, plus a dulcimer-maker, a printmaker, a spatter painter, two sculptors, and a watering hole called The Barre. This is one of those quiet little bistros where you aren't driven crazy by the constant ringing of cash registers. A nice place to drink but you wouldn't want to own it.

I hung up the phone and sat for a few minutes eyeballing an old nine-by-twelve glossy of myself, trying to get inspired. It's not a bad likeness. Blue pin-striped suit, a headful of hair, and I'm looking straight into 1965 like I owned it, and as for my line of work at the time, any one who has read *The Blonde in 204, Close Before Striking, The Big Tipper,* and *The Mark of a Heel* knows that I wasn't big on ballet.

I wasn't real smart at spotting trends, either. The private-eye business was getting thinner than sliced beef at the deli. I spent my days supporting a bookie and my nights tailing guys who weren't going anywhere anyway. My old pals in Homicide were trading in their wing tips and porkpie hats for Frye boots and Greek fisherman caps and growing big puffs of hair around their ears. Mine was the only suit that looked slept in. I felt like writing to the Famous Shamus School and asking what was I doing wrong.

"It's escapism, Mr. Schmidt," quavered Ollie, the elevator boy, one morning when I complained that nobody needed a snoop anymore. "I was reading in the *Gazette* this morning where they say this is an age of anti-intellectualism. A sleuth like yourself, now, you represent the spirit of inquiry, the scientific mind, eighteenth-century enlightenment, but heck, people don't care about knowing the truth anymore. They just want to have *experiences*."

"Thanks for the tip, Ollie," I smiled, flipping him a quarter. "And keep your eyes open."

I was having an experience myself at the time and her name was Trixie, an auburn-haired beauty who moved grown men to lie down in her path and wave their arms and legs. I was no stronger than the rest, and when she let it be known one day that the acting studio where she studied nights was low on cash and might have to close and thus frustrate her career, I didn't ask her to type it in triplicate. I got the dough. I learned then and there that true artists are sensitive about money. Trixie took the bundle and the next day she moved in with a sandalmaker. She said I wasn't her type. Too materialistic.

Evidently I was just the type that every art studio, mime troupe, print gallery, folk-ballet company, and wind ensemble in town was looking for, though, and the word got around fast: Jack Schmidt knows how to dial a telephone and make big checks arrive in the mail. Pretty soon my outer office was full of people with long delicate fingers, waiting to tell me what marvelous, marvelous things they could do if only they had ten thousand dollars (minus my percentage). It didn't take me long to learn the rules—about twenty minutes. First rule: ten thousand is peanuts. Pocket money. Any arts group that doesn't need a hundred grand and need it *now* just isn't thinking hard enough.

My first big hit was a National Endowment for the Arts grant for a walk-up tap school run by a dishwater blonde named Bonnie Marie Beebe. She also taught baton, but we stressed tap on the application. We called the school The American Conservatory of Jazz Dance. A hundred and fifty thousand clams. "Seed money" they called it, but it was good crisp lettuce to me.

I got the Guild of Younger Poets fifty thousand from the Teamsters to produce some odes to the open road, and another fifteen from a lumber tycoon with a yen for haiku. I got a yearlong folk-arts residency for a guy who told Scandinavian jokes, and I found wealthy backers for a play called *Struck by Lightning*, by a non-literalist playwright who didn't write a script but only spoke with the director a few times on the phone.

Nobody was too weird for Jack Schmidt. In every case, I had met weirder on the street. The Minnesota Anti-Dance Ensemble, for example, is a bunch of sweet kids. They simply don't believe in performance. They say that "audience" is a passive concept, and they spend a lot of time picketing large corporations in protest against the money that has been given to them, which they say comes from illicit profits. It doesn't make my life easier, but heck, I was young once, too. Give me a choice, I'll take a radical dance group over a Renaissance-music ensemble any day. Your average shawm or sackbut player thinks the world owes him a goddamn living.

So I was off the pavement and into the arts, and one day Bobby Jo walked in, fresh out of St. Cloud State Normal and looking for money to teach interior decorating to minority kids, and she saw I needed her more. She threw out my electric fan and the file cabinet with the half-empty fifth in the third drawer and brought in some Mondrian prints and a glass-topped desk and about forty potted plants. She took away my .38 and made me switch to filter cigarettes and had stationery printed up that looks like it's recycled from beaten eggs. "Arts Consultant," it says, but what I sell is the same old hustle and muscle, which was a new commodity on the arts scene then.

"What your arts organizations need is a guy who can ask people for large amounts without blushing and twisting his hankie," I told her one day, en route to Las Palmas for a three-day seminar on the role of the arts in rural America. "Your typical general manager of an arts organization today is nothing but a bagman. He figures all he has to do is pass the hat at the board meeting and the Throttlebottoms will pick up the deficit. The rest of the time he just stands around at lawn parties and says witty things. But the arts are changing, Bobby Jo. Nowadays, everybody wants arts, not just the rich. It's big business. Operating budgets are going right through the ceiling. All of a sudden, Mr. Arts Guy finds the game has changed. Now he has to work for the money and hit up corporations and think box office and dive in and fight for a slice of the government pie, and it scares him right out of his silk jammies. That's when he calls for Schmidt."

She slipped her hand into mine. I didn't take her pulse or anything, but I could tell she was excited by the way her breath came in quick little gasps.

"Now anyone who can spell 'innovative' can apply for a grant, government or otherwise," I went on, "but that doesn't mean that the bozo who reads the application is necessarily going to bust into tears and run right down to Western Union. He needs some extra incentive. He needs to know that this is no idle request for funds typed up by somebody who happened to find a blank application form at the post office. He needs to know that you are counting on the cash, that you fully expect to get it, and that if you are denied you are capable of putting his fingers in a toaster. The arts are growing, Bobby Jo, and you and me are going to make it happen."

"You are a visionary, J.S.," she murmured. "You have a tremendous overall concept but you need a hand when it comes to the day-to-day."

"Speaking of ideas," I muttered hoarsely, and I pulled the lap blanket up over our heads. She whispered my initials over and over in a litany of passion. I grabbed her so hard her ribs squeaked.

It was a rough morning. After Bobby Jo's phone call, I got another from the Lawston Foundry, informing me that Stan Lewandowski's sculpture, *Oppresso*, would not be cast in time for the opening of the Minot Performing Arts Center. The foundry workers, after hearing what Lewandowski was being paid for creating what looked to them like a large gerbil cage, went out on strike, bringing the sculpture to a standstill. I wasted fifteen minutes trying to make a lunch date with Hugo Groveland, the mining heir, to discuss the Arts Mall. He was going away for a while, Groveland said, and didn't know when he'd be back, if ever. He hinted at dark personal tragedies that were haunting him and suggested I call his mother. "She's more your type," he said, "plus she's about to kick off, if you know what I mean."

On top of it, I got a call from the director of our dinner theatre in upstate Indiana. He had been irked at me for weeks since I put the kibosh on *Hedda Gabler*. He had been plumping for a repertory theatre. "Fine," I said. "As long as you make it *Fiddler on the Roof*, *The Sunshine Boys*, and *Man of La Mancha*." Now he was accusing us of lacking a commitment to new writers. He said I was in the business of exploiting talent, not developing it.

"Listen, pal," I snarled. "As a director, you'd have a hard time getting people to act normal. So don't worry about me exploiting your talent. Just make sure you have as many people in the cast as there are parts. And tell your kitchen to slice the roast beef thin."

So he quit. I wished I could, too. I had a headache that wouldn't. And an Arts Mall with twenty-four hours to live.

"It's a whole trend called the New Naiveté," offered Ollie when I asked him why artists seemed to hate me, on the way down to lunch. "I was reading in the *Gazette* where they say people nowadays think simplicity is a prime virtue. They want to eliminate the middleman. That's you, Mr. Schmidt. Traditionally, your role has been that of a buffer between the individual and a cruel world. But now people think the world is kind and good, if only they could deal with it directly. They think if they got rid of the middleman—the bureaucracy, whatever you call it—then everything would be hunky-dory."

"Thanks, Ollie," I said as the elevator doors opened. "Let's have lunch sometime."

It reminded me of something Bobby Jo had said in a taxicab in Rio, where we were attending a five-day conference on the need for a comprehensive system of evaluating arts information. "It's simple, J.S.," she said. "The problem is overhead. Your fat cats will give millions to build an arts center, but nobody wants to donate to pay the light bill because you can't put a plaque on it. They'll pay for Chippewa junk sculpture, but who wants to endow the janitor?"

"Speaking of endowments," I whispered hoarsely, and I leaned over and pressed my lips hungrily against hers. I could feel her earlobes trembling helplessly.

The mining heir's mother lived out on Mississippi Drive in a stone pile the size of the Lincoln Monument and about as cheerful. The carpet in the hall was so deep it was like walking through a swamp. The woman who opened the door eyeballed me carefully for infectious diseases, then led me to a sitting room on the second floor that could've gone straight into the Cooper-Hewitt Museum. Mrs. Groveland sat in a wing chair by the fireplace. She looked pretty good for a woman who was about to make the far turn.

"Mr. Smith, how good of you to come," she tooted, offering me a tiny hand. I didn't correct her on the name. For a few grand. I'm willing to be called a lot worse. "Sit down and tell me about your arts center," she continued. "I'm all ears."

So were the two Dobermans who sat on either side of her chair. They looked as if they were trained to rip your throat if you used the wrong fork.

Usually, my pitch begins with a description of the long lines of art-starved inner-city children bused in daily to the Arts Mall to be broadened. But the hounds made me nervous—they maintained the most intense eye contact I have ever seen from floor level—so I skipped ahead to the money part. I dropped the figure of fifty thousand dollars.

She didn't blink, so I started talking about the Mall's long-range needs. I mentioned a hundred thou. She smiled as if I had asked for a drink of water.

I crossed my legs and forged straight ahead. "Mrs. Groveland," I radiated, "I hope you won't mind if I bring up the subject of estate planning."

"Of course not," she radiated right back. "The bulk of my estate, aside from the family bequests and a lump-sum gift to the Audubon Society, is going for the care of Luke and Mona here." At the word "estate," the Dobermans seemed to lick their chops.

I had to think fast. I wasn't about to bad-mouth our feathered friends of the forest, or Mrs. Groveland's family, either, but I thought I just might shake loose some of the dog trust. I told her about our Founders Club for contributors of fifty thousand or more. Perhaps she could obtain *two* Founderships—one for each Doberman. "Perhaps it would take a load off your mind if you would let us provide for Luke and Mona," I said. "We could act as their trustees. We just happen to have this lovely Founders Club Kennel, way out in the country, where—"

At the mention of a kennel, the beasts lowered their heads and growled. Their eyes never left my face.

"Hush, hush," Mrs. Groveland scolded gently. "Don't worry," she assured me, "they don't bite."

They may not bite, I thought, but they can sue.

Then Mona barked. Instantly, I was on my feet, but the dogs beat me to it. The sounds that came from their throats were noises that predated the Lascaux Cave paintings. They were the cries of ancient Doberman souls trying to break through the thin crust of domestication, and they expressed a need that was far deeper than that of the Arts Mall, the arts in general, or any individual artist whom I would care to know. The next sound I heard was the slam of a paneled oak door closing. I was out in the hallway and I could hear Mrs. Groveland on the other side saying, "*Bad* Luke, *naughty* Mona!" The woman who had let me in let me out. "They're quite protective," she informed me, chuckling. If a jury had been there to see her face, I'd have altered it.

When I got back to the office, I gathered up every piece of correspondence in our National Arts Endowment file and threw it out the window. From above, it looked like a motorcade was due any minute. I was about to follow up with some of the potted plants when the phone rang. It rang sixteen times before I picked it up. Before Bobby Jo could identify herself, I'd used up all the best words I know. "I'm *out*," I added. "Through. Done. Kaput. Fini. The End. Cue the creditors. I've had it."

"J.S.," she began, but I was having none of it.

"I've had a noseful of beating money out of bushes so a bunch of sniveling wimps can try the patience of tiny audiences of their pals and moms with subsidized garbage that nobody in his right mind would pay Monopoly money to see," I snapped. "I'm sick of people calling themselves artists who make pots that cut your fingers when you pick them up and wobble when you set them on a table. I'm tired of poets who dribble out little teensy poems in lower-case letters and I'm sick of painters who can't even draw an outline of their own hand and I'm finished with the mumblers and stumblers who tell you that if you don't understand them it's *your* fault."

I added a few more categories to my list, plus a couple dozen persons by name, several organizations, and a breed of dog.

"You all done, J.S.?" she asked. "Because I've got great news. The Highways Department is taking the Arts Mall for an interchange. They're ready to pay top dollar, plus—you won't believe this—to sweeten the deal, they're throwing in six point two miles of Interstate 594."

"Miles of what?" Then it clicked. "You mean that unfinished leg of 594?" I choked.

"It's been sitting there for years. There are so many community groups opposed to it that the Highways Department doesn't dare cut the grass that's growing on it. They want us to take them off the hook. And if we make it an arts space, they figure it'll fulfill their beautification quota for the next three years."

"We'll call it The ArtsTrip!" I exclaimed. "Or The ArtStrip! The median as *medium!* Eight-lane environmental art! Big, big sculptures! Action painting! Wayside dance areas! Living poetry plaques! Milestones in American music! Arts parks and Arts lots! A drive-in film series! The customized van as Artsmobile! People can have an arts experience without even pulling over onto the shoulder. They can get quality enrichment and still make good time!"

"Speaking of making time—" Her voice broke. She

shuddered like a turned-on furnace. Her breath came in sudden little sobs.

I don't know what's next for Jack Schmidt after the Arts Highway is finished, but, whatever it is, it's going to have Jack Schmidt's name on it. No more Mr. Anonymous for me. No more Gray Eminence trips for yours truly. A couple of days ago, I was sitting at my desk and I began fooling around with an ink pad. I started making thumb-prints on a sheet of yellow paper and then I sort of smooshed them around a little, and one thing led to another, and when I got done with it I liked what I saw. It wasn't necessarily something I'd hang on a burlap wall with a baby ceiling-spot aimed at it, but it had a certain *definite* quality that art could use a lot more of. I wouldn't be too surprised if in my next adventure I'm in a loft in SoHo solving something strictly visual while Bobby Jo throws me smoldering looks from her loom in the corner. In the meantime, good luck and stay out of dark alleys.

Garrison Keillor. *Happy to Be Here.* NY: Penguin, 1983.

Bret Harte

The Stolen Cigar Case

To literature's dying day, Francis Bret Harte will be known as the author of those sentimental burlesques of California in the Gold Rush days, "The Outcasts of Poker Flat" and "The Luck of Roaring Camp," both of which appeared in Harte's first collection of short stories in 1870. And why not? They were some of the first great vernacular works on the west. They made Harte famous, sought after, arrogant, and unpredictable: everything, in fact, except rich. He spent the rest of his life churning out a staggering number of novels, plays, and stories of all kinds.

Like many writers he led a life of irony: his early stories of California made him so famous that he could leave California forever. Even more ironically, the world-renowned writer of Americana left America for good in 1878, to serve as U.S. Consul in Germany and later in Scotland. Many of his later stories of the deserts and mountains of old California were written while a member of the Royal Thames Yacht Club in the wild uncivilized reaches of London, England, where he lived the last seventeen years of his life.

Harte's stay in England coincided with the introduction, heyday, and death of one Mr. Sherlock Holmes. Sick of the attention Holmes received, Arthur Conan Doyle had killed off the detective in 1893, leaving a void of such staggering proportions that Doyle had to come up with a "pre-death" adventure, *The Hound of the Baskervilles,* in 1901. Just about that time Harte was busy writing a second series of "Condensed Novels"—the first series had been his very first book—burlesquing the popular writers of the day. With London all atwitter about the return of Holmes, Conan Doyle couldn't be ignored. And Harte, the master of plot, came up with a brilliant twist. Read on to find out what happens when Sherlock Holmes himself gets robbed!

* * *

I FOUND HEMLOCK JONES in the old Brook Street lodgings, musing before the fire. With the freedom of an old friend I at once threw myself in my usual familiar attitude at his feet, and gently caressed his boot. I was induced to do this for two reasons: one, that it enabled me to get a good look at his bent, concentrated face, and the other, that it seemed to indicate my reverence for his superhuman insight. So absorbed was he even then, in tracking some mysterious clue, that he did not seem to notice me. But therein I was wrong—as I always was in my attempt to understand that powerful intellect.

"It is raining," he said, without lifting his head.

"You have been out, then?" I said quickly.

"No. But I see that your umbrella is wet, and that your overcoat has drops of water on it."

I sat aghast at his penetration. After a pause he said carelessly, as if dismissing the subject: "Besides, I hear the rain on the window. Listen."

I listen. I could scarcely credit my ears, but there was the soft pattering of drops on the panes. It was evident there was no deceiving this man!

"Have you been busy lately?" I asked, changing the subject. "What new problem—given up by Scotland Yard as inscrutable—has occupied that gigantic intellect?"

He drew back his foot slightly, and seemed to hesitate ere he returned it to its original position. Then he answered wearily: "Mere trifles—nothing to speak of. The Prince Kupoli has been here to get my advice regarding the disappearance of certain rubies from the Kremlin: the Rajah of Pootibad, after vainly beheading his entire bodyguard, has been obliged to seek my assistance to recover a jeweled sword. The Grand Duchess of Pretzel-Brauntswig is desirous of discovering where her husband was on the night"—he lowered his voice slightly—"a lodger in this very house, meeting me on the stairs, wanted to know why they didn't answer his bell."

I could not help smiling—until I saw a frown gathering on his inscrutable forehead.

"Pray remember," he said coldly, "that it was through just such an apparently trivial question that I found out Why Paul Ferroll Killed His Wife, and What Happened to Jones!"

I became dumb at once. He paused for a moment, and then suddenly changing back to his usual pitiless, analytical style, he said: "When I say these are trifles, they are so in comparison to an affair that is now before me. A crime has been committed—and, singularly enough, against myself. You start," he said. "You wonder who would have dared to attempt it. So did I; nevertheless, it has been done. I have been *robbed!*"

"You robbed! You, Hemlock Jones, the Terror of Peculators!" I gasped in amazement, arising and gripping the table as I faced him.

"Yes! Listen. I would confess it to no other. But *you* who

have followed my career, who know my methods; you, for
whom I have partly lifted the veil that conceals my plans
from ordinary humanity—you, who have for years rap-
turously accepted my confidences, passionately admired
my inductions and inferences, placed yourself at my beck
and call, become my slave, groveled at my feet, given up
your practice except those few unremunerative and
rapidly decreasing patients to whom, in moments of ab-
straction over *my* problems, you have administered
strychnine for quinine and arsenic for Epsom salts; you,
who have sacrificed anything and everybody to me—*you* I
make my confidant!"

I arose and embraced him warmly, yet he was already so
engrossed in thought that at the same moment he mechan-
ically placed his hand upon his watch chain as if to consult
the time. "Sit down," he said. "Have a cigar?"

"I have given up cigar smoking," I said.

"Why?" he asked.

I hesitated, and perhaps colored. I had really given it up
because with my diminished practice, it was too expensive.
I could afford only a pipe. "I prefer a pipe," I said
laughingly. "But tell me of this robbery. What have you
lost?"

He arose, and planting himself before the fire with his
hands under his coat tails, looked down upon me reflec-
tively for a moment. "Do you remember the cigar case
presented to me by the Turkish ambassador for discovering
the missing favorite of the Grand Vizier in the fifth chorus
girl at the Hilarity Theater? It was that one. I mean the
cigar case. It was incrusted with diamonds."

"And the largest one had been supplanted by paste," I
said.

"Ah," he said, with a reflective smile, "you know that?"

"You told me yourself. I remember considering it a proof
of your extraordinary perception. But, by Jove, you don't
mean to say you have lost it?"

He was silent for a moment. "No: it has been stolen, it is

true, but I shall still find it. And by myself alone! In your profession, my dear fellow, when a member is seriously ill, he does not prescribe for himself, but calls in a brother doctor. Therein we differ. I shall take this matter in my own hands."

"And where could you find better?" I said enthusiastically. "I should say the cigar case is as good as recovered already."

"I shall remind you of that again," he said lightly. "And now, to show you my confidence in your judgment, in spite of my determination to pursue this alone, I am willing to listen to any suggestions from you."

He drew a memorandum book from his pocket and, with a grave smile, took up his pencil.

I could scarcely believe my senses. He, the great Hemlock Jones, accepting suggestions from a humble individual like myself! I kissed his hand reverently, and began in a joyous tone:

"First, I should advertise, offering a reward; I should give the same intimation in handbills, distributed at the 'pubs' and the pastry cooks'. I should next visit the different pawnbrokers; I should give notice at the police station. I should examine the servants. I should throroughly search the house and my own pockets. I speak relatively," I added, with a laugh. "Of course I mean *your* own."

He gravely made an entry of the details.

"Perhaps," I added, "you have already done this?"

"Perhaps," he returned enigmatically. "Now, my dear friend," he continued, putting the notebook in his pocket and rising, "would you excuse me for a few moments? Make yourself perfectly at home until I return: there may be some things," he added with a sweep of his hand toward his heterogeneously filled shelves, "that may interest you and while away the time. There are pipes and tobacco in that corner."

Then nodding to me with the same inscrutable face he

left the room. I was too well accustomed to his methods to think much of his unceremonious withdrawal, and made no doubt he was off to investigate some clue which had suddenly occurred to his active intelligence.

Left to myself I cast a cursory glance over his shelves. There were a number of small glass jars containing earthy substances, labeled PAVEMENT AND ROAD SWEEPINGS, from the principal thoroughfares and suburbs of London, with the subdirections FOR IDENTIFYING FOOT TRACKS. There were several other jars, labeled FLUFF FROM OMNIBUS AND ROAD-CAR SEATS, COCONUT FIBER AND ROPE STRANDS FROM MATTINGS IN PUBLIC PLACES, CIGARETTE STUMPS AND MATCH ENDS FROM FLOOR OF PALACE THEATRE, ROW A, 1 TO 50. Everywhere were evidences of this wonderful man's system and perspicacity.

I was thus engaged when I heard the slight creaking of a door, and I looked up as a stranger entered. He was a rough-looking man, with a shabby overcoat and a still more disreputable muffler around his throat and the lower part of his face. Considerably annoyed at this intrusion, I turned upon him rather sharply, when, with a mumbled, growling apology for mistaking the room, he shuffled out again and closed the door. I followed him quickly to the landing and saw that he disappeared down the stairs. With my mind full of the robbery, the incident made a singular impression upon me. I knew my friend's habit of hasty absences from his room in his moments of deep inspiration; it was only too probable that, with his powerful intellect and magnificent perceptive genius concentrated on one subject, he should be careless of his own belongings, and no doubt even forget to take the ordinary precaution of locking up his drawers. I tried one or two and found that I was right, although for some reason I was unable to open one to its fullest extent. The handles were sticky, as if someone had opened it with dirty fingers. Knowing Hemlock's fastidious cleanliness, I resolved to inform him of this circumstance, but I forgot it, alas! until—but I am anticipating my story.

His absence was strangely prolonged. I at last seated myself by the fire and, lulled by warmth and the patter of the rain, fell asleep. I may have dreamt, for during my sleep I had a vague semiconsciousness as of hands being softly pressed on my pockets—no doubt induced by the story of the robbery. When I came fully to my senses, I found Hemlock Jones sitting on the other side of the hearth, his deeply concentrated gaze fixed on the fire.

"I found you so comfortably asleep that I could not bear to awaken you," he said, with a smile.

I rubbed my eyes. "And what news?" I asked. "How have you succeeded?"

"Better than I expected," he said, "and I think," he added, tapping his notebook, "I owe much to *you.*"

Deeply gratified, I awaited more. But in vain. I ought to have remembered that in his moods Hemlock Jones was reticence itself. I told him simply of the strange intrusion, but he only laughed.

Later, when I arose to go, he looked at me playfully. "If you were a married man," he said. "I would advise you not to go home until you had brushed your sleeve. There are a few short brown sealskin hairs on the inner side of your forearm, just where they would have adhered if your arm had encircled a sealskin coat with some pressure!"

"For once you are at fault," I said triumphantly; "the hair is my own, as you will perceive; I have just had it cut at the barber shop, and no doubt this arm projected beyond the apron."

He frowned slightly, yet, nevertheless, on my turning to go he embraced me warmly—a rare exhibition in that man of ice. He even helped me on with my overcoat and pulled out and smoothed down the flaps of my pockets. He was particular, too, in fitting my arm in my overcoat sleeve, shaking the sleeve down from the armhole to the cuff with his deft fingers. "Come again soon!" he said, clapping me on the back.

"At any and all times," I said enthusiastically; "I only ask ten minutes twice a day to eat a crust at my office, and four hours' sleep at night, and the rest of my time is devoted to you always, as you know."

"It is indeed," he said, with his impenetrable smile.

Nevertheless, I did not find him at home when I next called. One afternoon, when nearing my own home, I met him in one of his favorite diguises—a long blue swallow tailed coat, striped cotton trousers, large turn-over collar, blacked face, and white hat, carrying a tambourine. Of course to others the disguise was perfect, although it was known to myself, and I passed him—according to an old understanding between us—without the slightest recognition, trusting to a later explanation. At another time, as I was making a professional visit to the wife of a publican at the East End, I saw him, in the disguise of a broken-down artisan, looking into the window of an adjacent pawnshop. I was delighted to see that he was evidently following my suggestions, and in my joy I ventured to tip him a wink; it was abstractedly returned.

Two days later I received a note appointing a meeting at his lodgings that night. That meeting, alas! was the one memorable occurrence of my life, and the last meeting I had with Hemlock Jones! I will try to set it down calmly, though my pulses still throb with the recollection of it.

I found him standing before the fire, with that look upon his face which I had seen only once or twice—a look which I may call an absolute concatenation of inductive and deductive ratiocination—from which all that was human, tender, or sympathetic was absolutely discharged. He was simply an icy algebraic symbol!

After I had entered he locked the doors, fastened the window, and even placed a chair before the chimney. As I watched these significant precautions with absorbing interest, he suddenly drew a revolver and, presenting it to my temple, said in low, icy tones:

"Hand over that cigar case!"

Even in my bewilderment my reply was truthful, spontaneous, and involuntary. "I haven't got it," I said.

He smiled bitterly, and threw down his revolver. "I expected that reply! Then let me now confront you with something more awful, more deadly, more relentless and convincing than that mere lethal weapon—the damning inductive and deductive proofs of your guilt!" He drew from his pocket a roll of paper and a notebook.

"But surely," I gasped, "you are joking! You could not believe—"

"Silence! Sit down!"

I obeyed.

"You have condemned yourself," he went on pitilessly. "Condemned yourself on my processes—processes familiar to you, applauded by you, accepted by you for years! We will go back to the time when you first saw the cigar case. Your expressions," he said in cold, deliberate tones, consulting his paper, "were, 'How beautiful! I wish it were mine.' This was your first step in crime—and my first indication. From 'I *wish* it were mine' to 'I *will* have it mine,' and the mere detail, '*How can* I make it mine?' the advance was obvious. Silence! But as in my methods it was necessary that there should be an overwhelming inducement to the crime, that unholy admiration of yours for the mere trinket itself was not enough. You are a smoker of cigars."

"But," I burst out passionately, "I told you I had given up smoking cigars."

"Fool!" he said coldly. "That is the *second* time you have committed yourself. Of course you told me! What more natural than for you to blazon forth that prepared and unsolicited statement to *prevent* accusation. Yet, as I said before, even that wretched attempt to cover up your tracks was not enough. I still had to find that overwhelming,

impelling motive necessary to affect a man like you. That
motive I found in the strongest of all impulses—love, I
suppose you would call it—" he added bitterly—"that
night you called! You had brought the most conclusive
proofs of it on your sleeve."

"But—" I almost screamed.

"Silence!" he thundered. "I know what you would say.
You would say that even if you had embraced some Young
Person in a sealskin coat, what had that to do with the
robbery? Let me tell you, then, that sealskin coat repre-
sented the quality and character of your fatal entangle-
ment! You bartered your honor for it—that stolen cigar
case was the purchaser of the sealskin coat!

"Silence! Having thoroughly established your motive, I
now proceed to the commission of the crime itself. Ordinary people would have begun with that—with an attempt
to discover the whereabouts of the missing object. These
are not *my* methods."

So overpowering was his penetration that, although I
knew myself innocent, I licked my lips with avidity to hear
the further details of this lucid exposition of my crime.

"You committed that theft the night I showed you the
cigar case, and after I had carelessly thrown it in that
drawer. You were sitting in that chair, and I had arisen to
take something from that shelf. In that instant you secured
your booty without rising. Silence! Do you remember when
I helped you on with your overcoat the other night? I was
particular about fitting your arm in. While doing so I
measured your arm with a spring tape measure, from the
shoulder to the cuff. A later visit to your tailor confirmed
that measurement. It proved to be *the exact distance between
your chair and that drawer!*" I sat stunned.

"The rest are mere corroborative details! You were again
tampering with the drawer when I discovered you doing
so! Do not start! The stranger that blundered into the
room with muffler on—was myself! More, I had placed a

little soap on the drawer handles when I purposely left you alone. The soap was on your hand when I shook it at parting. I softly felt your pockets, when you were asleep, for further developments. I embraced you when you left— that I might feel if you had the cigar case or any other articles hidden on your body. This confirmed me in the belief that you had already disposed of it in the manner and for the purpose I have shown you. As I still believed you capable of remorse and confession, I twice allowed you to see I was on your track: once in the garb of an itinerant Negro minstral, and the second time as a workman looking in the window of the pawnshop where you pledged your booty."

"But," I burst out, "if you had asked the pawnbroker, you would have seen how unjust—"

"Fool!" he hissed. "Do you suppose I followed any of your suggestions, the suggestions of the thief? On the contrary, they told me what to avoid."

"And I suppose," I said bitterly, "you have not even searched your drawer."

"No," he said calmly.

I was for the first time really vexed. I went to the nearest drawer and pulled it out sharply. It stuck as it had before, leaving a section of the drawer unopened. By working it, however, I discovered that it was impeded by some obstacle that had slipped to the upper part of the drawer, and held it firmly fast. Inserting my hand, I pulled out the impending object. It was the missing cigar case! I turned to him with a cry of joy.

But I was appalled at his expression. A look of contempt was now added to his acute, penetrating gaze. "I have been mistaken," he said slowly. "I had not allowed for your weakness and cowardice! I thought too highly of you even in your guilt! But I see now why you tampered with that drawer the other night. By some inexplicable means— possibly another theft—you took the cigar case out of pawn and, like a whipped hound, restored it to me in this feeble, clumsy fashion. You thought to deceive me, Hemlock Jones! More, you thought to destroy my infallibility. Go! I give you your liberty. I shall not summon the three policemen who wait in the adjoining room—but out of my sight forever!"

As I stood once more dazed and petrified, he took me firmly by the ear and led me into the hall, closing the door behind him. This reopened presently, wide enough to permit him to thrust out my hat, overcoat, umbrella, and overshoes, and then closed against me forever!

I never saw him again. I am bound to say, however, that thereafter my business increased, I recovered much of my old practice, and a few of my patients recovered also. I became rich. I had a brougham and a house in the West End. But I often wondered, if, in some lapse of consciousness, I had not really stolen his cigar case!

The Misadventures of Sherlock Holmes. Ed. by Ellery Queen. Boston: Little Brown, 1944.

John Harris

Monastic Mayhem:
An Echo of Eco

John Harris's career is a study in dualism. Take his masters' degrees: two, one in English from the University of Virginia and another in Italian from Berkeley in 1987. Take his editing jobs: two, with the Smithsonian Institution Press and now with the J. Paul Getty Museum in Malibu. His work, however, is singular.

A series of wickedly funny pieces from his pen left readers of *The Atlantic* in stitches in the late 1980s. His work has also appeared in *Esquire* and *Harper's*. Nothing yet in the '90s that I know of. Why not? Because, he says, "I haven't written anything new in a while—partly the result of middle-age slowness, partly because I'm permanently stunned by the beauty and sunshine of Southern California."

Pray for rain. Maybe that way we'll see more pieces like

this parody of that literary phenomenon, Umberto Eco. Labyrinthine, didactic, allusive, dense, and sometimes unreadable, his *The Name of the Rose* was the most unlikely of best sellers. Harris does the amazing job of boiling down the 600-plus pages of theological complexities of Eco's detective fable into a mere 2,000 words to uncover a murderer driven by intertextual impulses—and publishers' advances.

* * *

THOUGH I AM an old monk now, I have, I confess, had experiences. And among the experiences I shall never forget was a series of adventures involving my dear friend (dead of the plague these many years) Basil de Belge, a Dominican detective who, like me, was medieval. Together we helped solve the baffling crimes that occurred in 1329 at the Ecole Supérieure of the Abbé d'Alton, where, within twenty-four hours, approximately six terrible murders were committed. We arrived at Nones: by Matins things were hopping.

MATINS

"Basil," the Abbot said, grabbing my friend's arm in the cloister. "I will not mince words. Someone is dead who wasn't dead yesterday. I'm worried."

"I see," my friend replied. He stared into the distance. "A monk was found face down in the kitchen with a soup ladle in his hand and a paring knife in his back. He had been chopping garlic, though for some unaccountable reason there was about him the odor of roses."

"Basil!" the Abbot exclaimed. "You amaze me! How did you deduce all that from my simple words?""

"I found the body."

"Do you know who did it?"

"I have my suspicions, which are at the moment growing. Look for another corpse by Lauds."

I looked at my friend, lost in admiration. *I must write all this down,* I thought. *It will sell.*

LAUDS

While Basil was in the herb garden, ingesting herbs, the Abbot approached.

"Basil, I must speak with you."

"Yes?"

"Another body has been discovered. This time in the library."

"Who found the body?"

"Brother Marcel."

"I thought so. Can Brother Marcel read?"

"No, but he can write. An interesting case. He was a follower of the Flogensian heretics, then the Stalagmites. After that—"

"Spare me the dull details. Now tell me one thing: What time is it?"

"Seven-thirty, I mean, nearly Prime. Why?"

"Unless I am mistaken, we are too late. A third murder has been committed. And in Prime time." Basil laughed mirthlessly. "A joke in my country." He frowned. "Let me speak with the librarian."

"The librarian is dead."

"Oh."

"Would you care to speak to someone in the rare-book room?"

Basil snapped to attention. "The Abbé d'Alton *has* a rare-book room?"

"Of course."

"Then let me see it. At once. We haven't a moment to lose."

I looked at Basil, lost once again in admiration. *Boy*, I thought. *This will really sell.*

PRIME

After a quick tour of the rare-book room. Basil interviewed the rare-book librarian, one Brother Garcia of Marquez.

"Let us get to the point, Brother Garcia. Why is this rare-book room a place of evil and mystery? Why is it a veritable labyrinth of unspeakable horror?"

"May I reverently suggest that you have been reading too many books?"

"You think so? Then look in your card catalogue. Under *R*, as in rose."

Puzzled, Brother Garcia shuffled off into the stacks. A minute later we heard a bloodcurdling scream. Brother Garcia came running back to us.

"There's—there's—"

"A severed hand, wearing a rose-colored ring, filed under *R*? I thought so." Basil turned to me and smiled grimly. "And to think that the day is young," he said.

TERCE

The Abbott was frantic.

"What can we do. Basil? And of all times for such terrible things to be happening."

"Why do you say that?"

"Because at Sext the Inspector General of Écoles will be arriving. He is a personal enemy of mine, and a skilled controversialist and amateur detective."

"Who is this man? Perhaps I have heard of him."

"McKee of Spillano, the Irish-Italian Scourge of God. Whatever will we do?"

Basil frowned. "Let me ask you one thing, Reverend Father. Where were you between Prime and Terce?"

The Abbot thought for a moment. "Let me see...why yes. I was in the conservatorium with Colonel Mustard, a visiting English dignitary. Yes. As a matter of fact. I left him there."

"You left him there? Alone?"

"Yes, I did."

"Quickly. To the conservatorium."

The Abbott conducted us through several tortuous passages and unlikely twists. At last we arrived at a tiny door, which the Abbot unlocked with a huge, rusted key. He rushed inside. We waited "...two, three." Basil counted. Another bloodcurdling scream. The Abbot rushed out of the conservatorium, a look of horror on his face.

"Colonel Mustard is...is..."

"Dead." Basil said, helpfully. "Was there by any chance a piece of iron pipe by his head?"

"No," the Abbot said. "He had a noose around his neck. He was hanging from a curtain rod."

"A curtain rod?" I burst in. "That means a window!"

Basil gave me a withering look. "Would you say that this window was...bigger than a breadbox?"

"Oh, yes. Much bigger. In fact, it's a rose window."

"Ah." Basil said. "I begin to see the true nature of the criminal mind we are dealing with. Now go about your business, Reverend Father, and pretend that nothing has happened. Perhaps nothing *has* happened..." His voice trailed off. The Abbot and I exchanged puzzled glances. Then we took them back.

SEXT

At noon McKee of Spillano and his party arrived at the Abbé. Amid the fraternal embraces and ritual greetings an undercurrent of bottomless contempt set the tone. Basil kept in the background, and then wandered off to the herb garden, where he played his viola in the fog. I returned to my cell, where I fell asleep and dreamed a dream in vivid, voluminous detail. When I encountered Basil an hour later, I told him of it. "I don't believe a word of what you're saying. But of course!" he shouted, slapping his forehead. "Where is McKee?"

"The Abbot is taking him on a tour of the Abbé."

"We must get to the rare-book room before the Inspector General. Quickly!"

We arrived just as McKee and his party were entering the rare-book room. "Too late," Basil sighed. We heard a commotion and then cries for help. Inching through the crowd at the door, I peeked inside. There, slumped over the MAY I HELP YOU? sign, was Brother Garcia of Màrquez, with an arrow in his back. A rose was clenched between his teeth.

NONES

"You don't run a very tight ship here, do you, Abbot?"

"Please, Your Grace, you must allow me to—"

"Five murders in six hours. Pretty wild."

"Please, Your Grace. That's *four* murders," the Abbot sobbed. "Four murders and a severed hand."

"Details," the Inspector General snapped. "It looks like *I'm* going to have to get to the bottom of this."

"Reverend Father, Brother Basil de Belge is already—"

"Who? Basil de Belge? I've always wanted to meet that guy. I thought he'd gone over the Reichenbach Falls."

"I did disappear, Your Grace," Basil said, stepping forward. "But now I am back. And if I may be so bold, I would suggest you begin your investigation by finding the man with the missing hand. He should be easy to spot."

"Thanks, Brother Basil. When we need some advice, we'll know who to ask. Now, Abbot, call in the first witness."

"But, Your Grace," the Abbot said. "No one has seen anything."

"Call in someone, then."

As McKee began his interrogation, Basil and I retreated to the refectory.

Basil turned to me. "We must think. Dégleau, *think!*" My mind was blank. "Put yourself in the place of the murderer." I tried this, but the effort made me feel uncanny. "You are killing one monk for each of the canonical hours. Why?"

A thought struck me. "But Basil. It's nearly Vespers, and no one is dead yet. Perhaps—"

"That's it, Dégleau! It's now Nones! Between two and three o'clock! Two and three make five; a five-sided figure is a pentagon; Joachim of Fiore predicted that one day there would be a building known as the Pentagon that would be connected with unlimited wealth. The treasury of the Abbé! We must get there before the murderer!"

We didn't.

VESPERS

The treasurer of the Abbé d'Alton had been bashed in the head with a heavy, jewel-encrusted object that had, apparently, been designed as a murder weapon. And written on the wall, in blood, was the cryptic message "Eye-ah illed-kay e-thay onk-may. E-thay ose-ray." Basil studied the words closely. "Not traditional Latin," he said. "Or Greek. Not even Arabic, of which I know a smattering. Dégleau, I am beginning to wonder…" His voice trailed off, perhaps significantly.

As the monks carried away the body of the treasurer, Basil stood lost in thought. "Why do I kept thinking of flowers?" he asked. "Mother's Day is approaching," I ventured. In the ensuing silence. Basil tugged at his lower lip, then his upper lip, then both lips at once. "The library, Dégleau. Yes, the library. We must return to the library."

Since the librarian and the rare-book librarian were both dead, we had the place to ourselves. Basil pored over the precious volumes on the shelves, murmuring the Latin titles that were so meaningless to me. At last he pulled a book down and then stood for many minutes, reading by the fading light of the fourteenth-century sun. I stood watching. *Gosh*, I thought. *Maybe this* won't *sell.*

I wandered off into the labyrinth of the library, only to emerge in the laundry room. Ordinarily I would have been surprised to find a dead body in the laundry tub, but by now I was becoming hardened. In his lifeless hand was a piece of parchment with the single word *"sélavy"* scrawled across it. *C'est la vie?* I thought.

"Basil," I said, coming back into the library.

"Shhh," he said, not looking up. "I know."

COMPLINE

That evening the Abbot called a general meeting of the monks. McKee of Spillano was present too.

"How's the investigation?" he said, sneering at Basil. "Found out anything interesting?"

"As a matter of fact, I have," Basil replied.

McKee looked incredulous. "Such as?"

"Such as the solution to the murders at the Abbé d'Alton."

"Oh, yeah?"

"Yes."

There was a silence. Finally the Abbot broke down and began to scream hysterically. "For the love of God, then, Brother Basil, tell us who has committed this grisly string of murders. I mean, this string of grisly murders!"

Basil looked about the room. "It may come as something of a shock," he began deliberately, "given the fictiveness of our situation. But it just so happens that the murderer is none other than...*the person telling this story!* And by that I mean, none other than...*Dégleau!*"

For obvious reasons I immediately became the focus of attention in the crowded room. I laughed nervously, because I was nervous.

"Basil, don't be ridiculous! Why would I do such a thing?"

"I'm not entirely sure," Basil said. "Though I can tell you one thing: You got the idea from a book."

"Book?" I said. "What book?"

"A book in the rare-book room."

"Don't be ridiculous," I spluttered. "How could I—"

"Stop squirming, Dégleau. I saw the book with my own eyes; you checked it out only last month. A story of a murder in which the man telling the story commits the murder. Take him away."

"But, Basil." I screamed, as two monks grabbed my arms. "It's not true! It's a lie! I have never read such a book! Or even if I have, it was trash! What kind of a man do you take me for? No, you fools, I got the idea from—"

I stopped. Unfortunately, I had not stopped soon enough.

"Yes?" Basil said.

"All right," I said. "I got the idea from a book. But not *that* book. From a book written by a famous philosopher of language. An intellectual."

Basil looked incredulous. "Why would anyone read such a thing?" he asked. "Surely it would be boring?"

I hung my head. "Intertextual impulses," I said softly. "I have never been able to control them."

"*Eh bien,*" Basil said. "Intertextual impulses, indeed! They are the curse of the cursed times in which we live! When all one need," he said, tapping his forehead, "are the little gray brain cells!" And the last thing I saw was Basil de Belge tugging on his famous moustachios, which he prized so much, and which I previously forgot to mention.

Jon L. Breen

Breakneck

Stereotypes belong only, well, only between the covers of parodies. In real life they have a habit of making the stereotyper look foolish. So don't let Jon L. Breen's career as a reference librarian fool you; besides being a radio sports broadcaster and Vietnam vet, he's the finest parodist the mystery field ever produced.

Soon after earning a master's degree in library science, Breen in 1967 published in *Ellery Queen's Mystery Magazine* the first of some two dozen delicious parodies of every top name in mysteries, from Ellery Queen himself to John Dickson Carr, Agatha Christie, and John D. MacDonald with side jaunts along the way for Frank Merrivale and Charlie Chan. Breen also introduced a couple of series characters of his own for some later wise guy to parody and has written a mystery novel a year since the mid-eighties.

I could have picked any number of Breen's parodies, but "Breakneck" is special. For one thing, I still don't know of any other major (or even minor) humorist who has parodied Dick Francis. (Corrections cheerfully solicited.) And Breen did it at a time (written 1972, published 1973) when Francis and his string of hard-luck jockey heroes were known only to mystery aficionados instead of being world-famous veterans of the best seller lists. For those who like in-jokes, note that Francis's *Bonecrack* was his most recent novel when "Breakneck" was written. And cast a sly eye over the occupation of the pain-racked hero.

* * *

A Dick Francis "miniature novel"

LYING IN THE MUD, before the Colonel's chestnut clipped me with his right foreleg and knocked me senseless, I thought about Trudy Abbot's remark about small men always having to prove something. When I awoke in hospital, I had to pinch myself to prove I was alive. Moments later the arrows of pain in every fiber of my body made such a test unnecessary. I was alive and looking into Rud Mosby's scowling face.

I winced with the pain but got no sympathy.

"Wot happened?" he demanded.

"That gelding's no jumper, that's all."

"Don't tell me that! I've been training jumpers thirty years, and that's a jumper."

"Shadows he jumps, but fences are a bit of a sticky wicket for him. Did he come through all right?"

"He came through better than you. But we shot him anyway."

"Oh. It was the Colonel's chestnut got me with his right fore."

"I know. The jockey claimed interference against your bloody head."

"Did the stewards allow it?"

"No, but you're suspended for a fortnight. And you'll never ride for me again, I can tell you."

Trudy came later. "Have to ride them, don't you?"

"It's my work."

"A certified librarian, and you have to ride those damned jumpers. Little men always have to prove something. I fancy you fell off that horse and got kicked just so I'd come running and say I loved you. True, isn't it?"

"I wanted to stay on and win."

"Huh! A lot you care about how I feel. And a certified librarian you are, too."

"I can't be around books all day. I have a dust allergy."

"You'll never change. Give us a little kiss."

"I can't move. I'm in great pain."

"Little men always have to prove something," she said, and walked out.

At midnight after the night nurse had gone, three big blokes came into my room and beat me senseless with truncheons and riding crops. Nobody heard my screams and they found me in the morning. I was a bloody mess and a bit of an embarrassment to a tour going round the hospital.

At noon they discharged me, but I couldn't get any horses to ride at the Cleckheaton races. None of the trainers would talk to me. Soon I remembered I was sent down for a fortnight and I went to fly my plane. I smashed up in a cornfield and the farmer chased me off with a pitchfork. I brought back the local bobby from the next town, riding on his crossbar, but all traces of my plane wreckage were gone. It made me a bit suspicious.

I went to see Trudy and told her things were not going well for me. She put me to work cataloguing her library. I had a sneezing fit. She said I was disgusting and told me to go away.

As soon as I stepped out of the door I saw the three blokes who'd beat me up. They took off in a Jaguar. I stole a horse from the stable and followed them to the farm where I'd crashed my plane.

I'd picked the horse at random, but he was more of a jumper than the crab that Rud Mosby had put me on the day before. He took the fences well but not too quietly. The three blokes saw me coming, and soon they came after me with their riding crops and truncheons, the farmer following closely with his pitchfork.

Knocked off my mount, I noticed his right fore hoof. It was the Colonel's chestnut. I should have recognized him before. Then Trudy knew the Colonel!

The chestnut helped me fight them off, flailing his hooves, as a good jumper will. I tied them all to the farmer's privy and took off for the Cleckheaton racecourse.

The trap was laid at the fourth fence. I could see them in the distance, the three crouched figures lurking behind the fence, hidden from the view of the riders and from the stands far in the distance.

I joined the field on the flat and surged to the front. The chestnut's ears twitched competitively. The stands were too far away for them to tell I was an interloper, though I had no silks on, only my flying togs. The other riders noticed, and shouted at me, but I pulled away from them. I had to reach that jump first.

The chestnut took the jump beautifully. At the height of his soaring leap, just as he cleared the fence, I dived from his back and wrestled with the three hidden figures: Rud Mosby, the Colonel, Trudy Abbot.

"All in it together, were you?" I cried. "Your horse betrayed you, Colonel, like a good jumper will."

I threw them all in a pile, clear of the charging field, but as the seventeen of them cleared the fence, a big bay mare clipped me with her left fore and knocked me senseless.

Waking up in hospital, aching in every bone, I told a Scotland Yard man about the plot to end racing in Britain forever. He assured me Trudy, Mosby, the Colonel, the farmer, and the three blokes were all safely rounded up.

The Colonel's chestnut was cited by the Jockey Club for heroism.

I was warned off for life.

It gives me lots of time to fly.

Ellery Queen's Mystery Magazine. Feb. 1973.

Robert Benchley

The Mystery of the Poisoned Kipper

Great humorists seem to be multitalented, or perhaps it's just that their talents are demanded in so many fields. Robert Benchley's wit could be found at various times in his work as a drama critic, book reviewer, press analyst, noted after-dinner speaker, radio star, Broadway personality, and as the winner of an Academy Award for best short subject of the year. Little wonder he was once described as "all things to all men—and all of them funny."

Benchley stories are legend (often a very good term for them, too). His relations with his bank may be guessed by the checks he endorsed, "Dear Banker's Trust, I love you. Bob." The office he once shared with Dorothy Parker was so small that he is supposed to have said, "If it were any smaller, it would have constituted adultery."

Humorous shorts are never played in the movies any-more (why not?, he asked) and yesterday's radio stars are nostalgia at best. Benchley lives on in the hundreds of humor pieces collected in books with such marvelous names as *From Bed to Worse; or, Comforting Thoughts About the Bison, After 1903—What?*, and that bane of librarians, *20,000 Leagues Under the Sea; or, David Copperfield.*

Though the kindliest of men, Benchley shared the humorist's hatred of pretension, and so his parodies—on targets as varied as Ernest Hemingway, Robert Louis Stevenson, and letter writers to English newspapers—are still sharp and witty today.

"The Mystery of the Poisoned Kipper" takes apart the rigidly formal school of the English whodunits, too many of which seem to feature a very proper ex-Army man, bizarre clues, and motiveless crimes. All grist for the mill of Mr. Benchley's very proper brand of purest nonsense.

* * *

WHO SENT THE POISONED KIPPER to Major General Han-nafield of the Royal Welch Lavaliers? That is the problem which is distorting Scotland Yard at the present moment, for the solution lies evidently in the breast of Major General Hannafield himself. And Major General Han-nafield is dead. (At any rate, he doesn't answer his telephone.)

Following are the details, such as they are. You may take them or leave them. If you leave them, please leave them in the coat room downstairs and say that Martin will call for them.

One Saturday night about three weeks ago, after a dinner given by the Royal Welch Lavaliers for the Royal Platinum Watch, Major General Hannafield returned home just in time for a late breakfast which he really didn't want. In fact, when his wife said, rather icily, "I suppose you've had your breakfast," the Maj. Gen. replied: "I'll thank you not to mention breakfast, *or* lunch, *or* dinner, until such time as I give you the signal." Mrs. Hannafield thereupon packed her bags and left for her mother's in New Zealand.

Along about eleven thirty in the morning, however, the Maj. Gen. extricated himself from the hatrack where he had gone to sleep, and decided that something rather drastic had to be done about his mouth. He thought of getting a new mouth; but as it was Sunday all the mouth shops were closed, and he had no chance of sending into London for anything. He thought of water, great tidal waves of water, but even that didn't seem to be exactly adequate. So naturally his mind turned next to kippered herring. "Send a thief to catch a thief," is an old saying but a good one, and applies especially to Sunday-morning mouths.

So he rang for his man, and nobody answered.

The Maj. Gen. then went to the window and called out to the gardener, who was wrestling with a dahlia, and suggested that he let those dahlias alone and see about getting a kipper, and what's more a very salty kipper, immediately. This the gardener did.

On receiving the kipper, the Maj. Gen., according to witnesses, devoured it with avidity, paper and all, and then hung himself back up on the hatrack. This was the last that was seen of Major General Hannafield alive, although perhaps "alive" is too strong a word. Perhaps "breathing" would be better.

Mrs. Hannafield, being on her way to New Zealand, has been absolved of any connection with the crime (if causing the Maj. Gen.'s death can be called a crime, as he was quite an offensive old gentleman). The gardener, from his cell in the Old Bailey, claims that he bought the kipper from a fish stall in the High Street, and the fish vender in the High Street claims that he bought the kipper from the gardener.

According to the officials of Scotland Yard, there are two possible solutions to the crime, neither of them probable: revenge, or inadvertent poisoning of the kipper in preparation. Both have been discarded, along with the remainder of the kipper.

Revenge as a motive is not plausible, as the only people who could possibly seek revenge on the Maj. Gen. were killed by him a long time ago. The Maj. Gen. was notoriously hot-tempered, and, when opposed, was accustomed to settling his neck very low in his collar and rushing all the blood available to his temples. In such states as this he usually said: "Gad, sir!" and lashed out with an old Indian weapon which he always carried, killing his offender. He was always acquitted, on account of his war record.

It is quite possible that some relatives of one of the Maj. Gen.'s victims might have tracked him from the Punjab or the Kit-Kat Club to his "diggings" in Diggings Street, but he usually was pretty careful to kill only people who were orphans or unmarried.

There was some thought at first that the Maj. Gen. might have at one time stolen the eye of an idol in India and brought it back to England, and that some zealot had followed him across the world and wreaked vengeance on him. A study of the records, however, shows that the Maj. Gen. once tried to steal an emerald eye out of an Indian idol, but that the idol succeeded in getting the Maj. Gen.'s eye instead, and that the Maj. Gen. came back to England wearing a glass eye—which accounted for his baffling mannerism of looking over a person's shoulder while that person was talking to him.

Now as for the inadvertent poisoning of a kipper in the process of being cured, Herring are caught off the coast of Normandy (they are also caught practically everywhere, but Normandy makes a better story), brought to shore by

Norman fishermen dressed up as Norman fishermen, and carried almost immediately to the Kipperers.

The herring kipperers are all under state control and are examined by government agents both before and after kippering. They are subjected to the most rigid mental tests, and have to give satisfactory answers to such questions as "Do you believe in poisoning herring?" and "Which of the following statements is true? (*a*) William the Norman was really a Swede; (*b*) herring, placed in the handkerchief drawer, give the handkerchiefs that *je ne sais quoi;* (*c*) honesty is the best policy."

If the kipperers are able to answer these questions, and can, in addition, chin themselves twelve times, they are allowed to proceed with their work. Otherwise they are sent to the French Chamber of Deputies, or Devil's Island, for ten years. So you can see that there is not much chance for a herring kipperer to go wrong, and practically no chance for Major General Hannafield to have been poisoned by mistake.

This leaves really nothing for Scotland Yard to work on, except an empty stomach. The motive of revenge being out, and accidental poisoning being out, the only possible solution remaining is that Major General Hannafield was in no state to digest a kippered herring and practically committed suicide by eating it. This theory they are working on, and at the coroner's inquest (which ought to come along any day now) the whole matter will be threshed out.

An examination of the Maj. Gen.'s vital organs has disclosed nothing except a possible solution of the whereabouts of the collier Cyclops, which was lost during the Great War.

Here the matter stands, or rather *there*. (It was here a minute ago.) Mrs. Hannafield may have some suggestions to offer, if she ever will land in New Zealand, but, according to radio dispatches, she is having an awfully good time on the boat and keeps going back and forth without ever getting off when they put into port. She and the ship's doctor have struck up an acquaintance, and you know what that means.

Robert Benchley. *No Poems; or, Around the World Backwards and Sideways*. NY: Harper & Brothers, 1932.

Jim Davis and Ron Tuthill

Babes and Bullets

All right, maybe you'll scream if you see one more stuffed Garfield peering at you from the side window of a passing car or if you run across yet another piece of Garfield kitsch, like Garfield chopsticks. Think of the alternative: Jim Davis spent five years trying to peddle a Gnorm the Gnat strip before going on to America's favorite lasagne-loving cat.

There are no cats in Davis's house today (his wife is allergic to them) though he grew up on a farm with twenty-five "outside" felines. He apprenticed with the "Tumbleweeds" strip while collecting rejection slips for his own ideas. Garfield was the last in a nine-year series. It clicked.

The strip's debut on June 19, 1978, in forty-one newspapers allowed Davis to celebrate by buying a newer used car. By 1981 Garfield appeared in 450 newspapers, by 1984, 1700. Today he's in 2,000 papers in seven languages and twenty-two countries. A series of TV specials and literally thousands of licensed products followed. By now Davis, if cause for more celebration came along, could probably buy his hometown of Fairmont, Indiana (which he shares with James Dean), or even his adopted home of Muncie, where he and his staff work in a sprawling complex of buildings.

I'm shattering no illusions, I trust, by noting that creating a cartoon empire is not a solitary occupation. Davis usually does his own gag writing for the daily strips, but certainly much of what you see in Garfield's various incarnations comes from the fertile minds of Davis's huge staff. (Other cartoonists, set in their lonely ways, have on occasion made fun of the Davis menage.) "Babes and Bullets," in truth, started life completely Davisless. It was written by Ron Tuthill and had illustrations by Kevin Campbell in its original appearance in *Garfield: His 9 Lives*. With Garfield himself as the lead, Babes was turned into a television special and then given its own book in a slightly rewritten version. This is the original, though, a rare Garfield text piece and a fine spoof of all private eyes with—though Dashiell Hammett may not have appreciated it—possibly the funniest parody name of all time. Don't delay: start right in on "The Continuing Adventures of Sam Spayed."

* * *

THE DUST HAD TO BE AN INCH THICK on my desk. A thick layer of papers was forming around the base of the trash can. An empty bottle of scotch lay on the floor next to the couch where I had a business engagement the night before.

"Coffee, Sam?"

Kitty wasn't much on keeping an office clean, but she *could* make a great cup of coffee. I still remember the day she came in looking for work. The dust had to be a half inch thick on my desk. A thin layer of papers was forming around the base of the trash can. A half-empty bottle of scotch sat on the floor next to the couch where I had a business engagement the night before.

She wanted to be a secretary. She had all the require-ment—a great body that would make your back arch, and she made a great cup of coffee. I gave her a job. That was yesterday.

San Francisco is a beautiful city...the cable cars, fog rolling off the bay, Chinatown, the Golden Gate Bridge, the wharf. Gee, I wish I lived there.

Being a private dick isn't easy with a name like Sam Spayed. It takes a special breed to be in my line of work. The hours are long, the pay stinks, and you can't trust anyone. It's not a pretty job. But, I've got all the require-ments. I like babes and bullets...and, I look good in a trench coat.

"More coffee, Sam?"

It was a slow day. The hours seemed to drag by like a Cubs vs. Braves doubleheader. I decided to get a phone. As I was leaving the office, I found myself face-to-face with one of the most beautiful creatures I'd ever seen. Her ears were limpid pools of gray with coal black slits; her whiskers swayed in the brisk, city breeze like cattails on a frog pond in southern Louisiana in September...uh, where was I? Oh, yeah, the broad. She was cute.

"Are you Spayed?"

I never know how to answer that question.

So, why had she come to see me? What mysterious problem drove her to a Private Investigator? And, why me? There were a hundred Private Investigators in town with better offices than mine. Who was she? I decided to find out...

"So, what brings you here? And, why me? There are a

hundred P.I.'s in town with better offices than mine. Who are you?"

"My husband was murdered. You're cheap. Tanya O'Tabby. Will you take the case?"

I had to think for a min—"SURE!"

"How do you want your services paid, Mr. Spayed?"

"That would be great!"

My mind took off like a greyhound after a rabbit at Raceway Park. She *was* attractive and *young*. Judging from the way she was dressed, she was obviously tapping some big bucks. How would a girl get her hands on money like that? Of course! It all makes sense, now. She marries an old geezer, has him killed, and inherits all the money. She hires a second-rate investigator to find the killer, who she doublecrosses, and ends up scot free.

"So, how old was your husband, Mrs. O'Tabby?"

"Twenty-three."

Of course! It all makes sense, now. Her husband was obviously a ladies' man. He probably had felines in every alley. An Irish cat is known for his promiscuous nature. Tanya finds out he's unfaithful and has him snuffed. She hires a second-rate detective to find the killer, who she doublecrosses, and ends up scot free. It's one of the oldest shams in the book.

"So, what did your husband do for a living, Mrs. O'Tabby?"

"He was a priest."

Something wasn't right here.

"Wait a minute, doll. I thought priests weren't allowed to get married."

"He was Greek Orthodox, Mr. Spayed."

Of course, a Greek Orthodox priest named O'Tabby. It all made sense now.

"Call me Sam, please. What makes you think your husband was murdered?"

"He drove off Old Mountain Road, Sam Please. That's

forty miles away. He had no reason to be there. Besides, he was an excellent driver."

Her lips started to tremble. I took her paws in mine.

"Go home, kid. I've got work to do. I'll call when I've got something."

Why someone would murder a twenty-three-year-old priest was beyond me. Still, stranger things have happened in this town.

My first stop was the city morgue. It would be a few days before the funeral, so his body should still be in the condition it was when he was found. The entire story Tanya had told me sounded like nothing more than an unfortunate accident. But, her sincerity was no act. She believed that her husband was murdered. She didn't know how or why, but then, that's my job.

It was 11:00 A.M.

Walking up the steps to the morgue, I saw my old adversary. It was Lieutenant Theotis Washington. Everytime he crossed my path, it was bad luck. He was a black cat.

"Spayed! What brings you down here? Trying to find a client?"

"Sure Lieutenant. He's the one your blue boys shot in the back for J-walking."

"Watch it Spayed. I still have your license under investigation."

"Oh, yeah. Well, at least I know it's safe for awhile."

"Spayed, don't push me!"

"Wouldn't dream of it Lieutenant. Have a nice day!"

The Lieutenant was still saying goodbyes as I walked into the morgue. I spotted an old friend, Burt Fleebish. He'd been working there ever since I was a snotty-nosed kitten.

"Sam, what brings you down here?"

"Hey, Burt, I need to see a body."

"Who doesn't, eh, Sam? What's the name?"

"Father O'Tabby"

"Oh, yeah! Tough break...nice fella..."

"You knew him?"

"Oh, not really. I attended his church, St. Morris, for about the last six months. We'd talk occasionally after services."

I could tell Burt sort of liked the guy by the way he pulled out the drawer with the stiff.

Tabby looked like he'd been worked over by the Maulers of the Midway. It didn't surprise me. What was a guy supposed to look like when he goes through a guardrail fence, and down a mountain canyon in his car. If his body hadn't been thrown out of the car while it was rolling over, it would have been burned up when the car caught fire and exploded.

"When's the autopsy scheduled, Burt?"

"Autopsy, what autopsy?"

"His wife thinks it was murder, Burt."

"Murder! Sam, the man died in a disastrous car accident. It's as simple as that!"

"Burt, if things were as simple as that, I wouldn't have a job."

Looking down at O'Tabby, I noticed some yellowish-brown coloration on his chest and stomach hairs.

"Hey, Burt. Do you have any explanation for this?" I pointed out the pigment in question.

"Oh, could be almost anything—transmission fluid, brake fluid. Any kind of liquid from a car can make a stain like that."

"Do you have his clothes and any items he had on him when he was discovered?"

"Oh, sure, Sam. Right here.",

He handed me a plastic bag filled mostly with his torn, shredded and bloodstained clothes. I searched through the clothing looking for anything that might suggest murder. Right now, it looked as though poor O'Tabby just had a bad break on the mountain.

. His shirt was about the only item of clothing that was still recognizable, although it was badly ripped and blood-stained. I noticed the yellowish-brown stains were in the same location on the shirt that they were on the body. I had seen stains like this before. But, where? Maybe something would come to me later.

The pockets were empty, except for the stones and dirt from the fall down the mountain. There was a curious little stone in the vest pocket. It was very colorful on one side, almost as though it were painted.

The phone rang. As Burt went to answer it, I put the colorful stone in my pocket, I don't know why really. Maybe I just liked stones.

Burt hung up the phone and asked if there was anything else I needed before he put the body away.

"A clue, a motive, and a murderer. Goodnight Burt."

"Sam…"

"Yeah, Burt?"

"It's noon.

Next on the list was Father O'Tabby's church. I was still a couple of blocks from the church when I brushed by a big goon on the sidewalk with fists the size of babies. He grabbed me by the throat, drug me into a darkened alley and pounded me into next year. As I lay there in a crumpled heap, I smiled to myself. I must be on the trail of something hot to rate a beating from this Neanderthal. I put my jaw back in place and pointed an accusing paw at my assailant.

"So, Clyde…I suppose you have a message for me."

"Yeah. I'm your landlord. You're two months late with the rent."

"Right."

I was still trying to figure out my landlord's involvement in this caper, as I walked up the marble steps to the church. At the doorway, I was greeted by an elderly man wearing a robe.

"Are you the Father here?"

"Yes, but I have no children."

"What?"

"I'm sorry. That's a small, religious joke. Yes, I'm Father O'Felix. How may I help you?"

"I'm Sam Spayed, P.I." I held up my wallet.

"Nice wallet, Mr. P.I."

"I'd like to ask you a few questions about Father O'Tabby."

"Certainly, Mr. P.I. Why don't you come inside."

I entered the church and followed O'Felix to the kitchen. I sat at the table as the Father poured us a cup of coffee. I would have preferred to have my own cup.

"What would you like to know, Mr. P.I.?"

"Call me Sam. Was O'Tabby a good driver?"

"Oh, yes. He was a drivers' training instructor at Edison High in the summer months."

"Do you have any idea why O'Tabby was on the Old Mountain Road last Friday night?"

"Yes, he was going to visit Maudie O'Purr, one of our parishioners. She is a wealthy hermit who has been ailing of late."

"Why was he going there?"

"Maude is a big contributor to the church. Father O'Tabby called on her every Friday night to help in any way he could."

"Does anyone else know this?"

"It was Maudie's wish that no one know of his visits."

"Did he have any enemies you knew of, Father?"

"What are you getting at, Sam?"

"Just the facts, Father."

"Father O'Tabby was loved by everyone who knew him, especially the female parishioners."

"What do you mean by that?"

"Just that he was an attractive man, and it was natural for women to be attracted to him."

Of course!

"How old is Maudie O'Purr?"

"Ninety-three."

"Rats."

Father O'Felix shifted restlessly in his chair.

"Sam, I meant nothing carnal by my statement. However, on more than one occasion Father O'Tabby had to put a woman's feelings in perspective."

"So, you don't think he ever gave in to temptation?"

"Oh, no. His only weakness was coffee. I rarely saw him without a cup of it in his hand."

"Yeah. Well, I think we all depend on a cup of Joe every now and then."

"Thanks for the information. And, no offense intended, but *this* is really lousy coffee."

"Yes, I admit my coffee needs work. Sam. The lady that normally makes our coffee left us recently. She made excellent coffee. She's going to be hard to replace. In fact, I find myself doing her duties more often than my own."

"I see. Well, nice meeting you."

It was only a few blocks back to my office. By the time I arrived, the men from the phone company had just installed my phone and were on their way out. Kitty was in the other room.

"No calls yet, Sam. How about a cup of coffee?"

I sat down at my desk and stared at the phone. I thought I'd better call Tanya and let her know the progress on the case. Maybe she could give me something else to go on.

"Hey, Kitty. Do we have Tanya's phone number?"

"555-1234, Sam."

"Thanks."

The girl might not be a great office cleaner, but she has a great memory. But, why didn't I remember that number? It's sure an easy one to remember.

"Hello, Tanya...Sam Spayed."

"Mr. Spayed, what did you find out?"

"Not much, really. Look, I stopped by your husband's church today and found out a few interesting things."

"Oh really, who did you talk with?"

"A Father O'Felix...do you know him?"

"Of course, Father O'Felix was my husband's assistant."

"Kind of old to be an assistant, isn't he?"

"Oh, we really never thought of him as an assistant. He worked as hard as my husband with the congregation. In fact, he's been with the church all his life."

Kitty was setting the cup of coffee down on my desk.

"Well, anyway, Tanya. He mentioned your husband may have had some woman trouble at the church and..."

CRASH!

"Damn it. That's hot!"

Kitty had dropped the cup of coffee on my desk and into my lap. It was hot enough to give a literal meaning to my last name. The cup had broken into several pieces on the desk.

"Sam, hello, Sam are you okay?"

"Look, Tanya, I'll call you back. We've got a bit of a mess right now."

I hung up.

"Sam, I'm so sorry! I don't know what I was thinking about."

"It's okay, Kitty. Run downstairs and tell maintenance we need a mop and bucket. I'll pick up the pieces of the mug."

I could tell she was really upset about the mess. Hell, it

was only coffee. Anyone can make a mistake. No problem. I'd fire her when she came back.

I was soaked. I went to the sink to clean up. As I took off my vest, I saw a huge coffee stain covering my shirt. Wait a minute! Coffee stains! That's what they were. O'Tabby had coffee stains on his shirt! Why would a man that was dressed as impeccably as O'Tabby wear a coffee-stained shirt? Where did the coffee come from? *And,* why am I talking to myself? I searched my vest pockets for the pretty, painted stone I took from O'Tabby's vest pocket. I looked at it carefully. It was painted, alright...a painted piece of ceramic! A piece of ceramic from a coffee cup! O'Tabby must have been drinking coffee, which in turn caused the accident. It wasn't much to go on. How was I supposed to solve a murder when my only clue was a cup of java?

What was keeping Kitty? Funny, she didn't seem to be the awkward type. I figured I'd better call Tanya to apologize for the interruption and to get back to the case. Where did I put the phone number? Wait a minute. Tanya never gave me a phone number. So, how did Kitty know the number? Easy, Spayed, don't go off the deep end. But, the pieces were starting to fit together. Kitty would know the number if Tanya's *husband* gave it to her. Could she be one of the felines infatuated with Father O'Tabby that Father O'Felix mentioned? Think Spayed, think. Of course! She spilled the coffee when I mentioned talking to Father O'Felix about O'Tabby's woman trouble. Kitty makes a great cup of coffee. So did the girl who recently left the church. The same girl I hired only yesterday. A girl who was infatuated by a man she could never have.

So, what does she do? She spills coffee in his lap and drives him over a cliff...something is not quite right here.

"Here's maintenance, Sam."

It was Kitty with an old tom cat carrying a pail and mop.

"I know you murdered Father O'Tabby, Kitty."

"What are you talking about, Sam?"

"You loved him, he didn't love you, you couldn't have him. So…you snuffed him."

She feel to her knees sobbing. "Yes, I loved him. He didn't love me, I couldn't have him, so I…"

"So you, what?"

"So I left."

"You left?"

"Yes, the thought of working at the church, so close to him and not being able to have him was too much to bear. So, I left. But, I didn't murder him."

The tears were streaming down her face and falling off her whiskers like rain off a pine tree.

"But, the coffee stains…the painted piece of ceramic coffee cup?" I held the ceramic piece out to her quivering paws.

"We talked a few nights before his death at the church. We had some coffee." The crying stopped. "He liked my coffee."

I had to agree with O'Tabby. Kitty made a great cup of coffee.

"He always drank from his favorite mug, Sam." She took the ceramic piece from my paw. "This looks like a piece from that mug. I don't know how it got broke."

I just ran out of suspects.

"Kitty, did you have any duties at the church other than making coffee?"

"I was Father O'Tabby's Girl Friday."

"You certainly weren't his Girl Saturday."

"Put a cork in it, Sam."

"Sorry."

"I sorted out his mail, answered the phone, filled his prescriptions, cleaned his robes…"

"Wait a minute! Filled his prescription?!"

"Yes, Father O'Tabby was an insomniac. The coffee kept him awake. He needed very potent sleeping pills to help him doze off at night."

Her expression softened to a sweet smile as she gazed into the distance.

"I remember him bragging that one of those pills could knock out a bull elephant. It took two to put him to sleep, and that took an hour."

"Kitty, stay here and help maintenance clean up this mess."

"Where are you going, Sam?"

"To pick up a murderer, baby."

I was packing my piece, although I didn't think I'd need it this time. It was pouring rain when I got outside. No matter, I was only going a few blocks.

The marble steps looked cold and gray—almost depressing. Not what you'd expect at the front of a church. It was 4:00 P.M.

When I found Father O'Felix, he was kneeling before the altar. His head was bowed and his paws clasped in prayer.

"Asking for forgiveness, Father?"

His head turned slowly. Wet streaks from his eyes to his mouth were on his furry face. It looked as though he had been crying for some time.

"I'm not worthy of being a Father," he continued sobbing.

"And, you don't have the equipment to be a mother."

"What?"

"Sorry, pal, that's a small, religious joke. Let's go."

By the time the paperwork was done, it was 8:00 P.M. Lt. Washington was his usual charming self, as O'Felix was being booked. It had been a long day. I thought I'd better check on Kitty. She was pretty shaken up when I left. As I walked back to the office, I noticed the rain had stopped...it was snowing. I entered my office and found Tanya O'Tabby sitting on the couch. She stood up slowly, sobbing, gently put her arms around me. She didn't say anything. She didn't have to. I understood. She stopped hugging me and smiled softly. She gave me an envelope and walked quietly out of my life.

"She called after you'd left." It was Kitty in the kitchen. "I told her you were going to nab the murderer. She came right over."

I didn't answer. My thoughts were still in the arms of a classy puss. There had better be a check in that envelope.

"Sam, how did you know Father O'Felix killed Father O'Tabby?"

"O'Tabby had to have left directly from the church to call on Maudie O'Purr that night, because he was still drinking from his favorite mug when the crash occurred. Father O'Felix, the substitute Girl Friday, fixed that cup of coffee. O'Felix had filled O'Tabby's sleeping pill prescription and popped a couple into his coffee knowing it would take O'Tabby an hour to get to Old Mountain Road 40 miles away. Like clockwork, O'Tabby fell asleep at the wheel and drove off the road. The motive was obvious."

"Which was?"

"It was the old, power struggle in the church routine, Kitty. Old man gets passed over by younger man. Young man gets power, notoriety, women, money. Old man gets older, bitter. Finally, out of frustration, the old man gets rid of only thing in his way...the young man. With O'Tabby gone, O'Felix becomes pastor and gets what has eluded him all his life."

Kitty came out of the kitchen holding a bottle of my favorite scotch and two glasses.

"Sam, you're simply too much." She closed the door to the office.

"What's the scotch for, Kitty?"

She set the bottle on the floor next to the couch and turned out the light.

Jim Davis. *Garfield: His Nine Lives.* NY: Ballantine, 1984.

Mr. Treet, Chaser of Lost People

After radio passed away, Bob Elliott and Ray Goulding resurrected it. The duo got their start on station WHDH in Boston in the late 1940s, just when the classic world of soap operas, westerns, cooking shows, wacky sportscasters, and ponderous editorial replies was being transferred to television—or strangled by it.

Bob & Ray spent countless hours in both mediums, but their comfortably baggy bodies and deadpan deliveries never quite worked as well on the tube. Besides, television viewers were apt to get confused by the type of minds which could kill off all the characters in one soap opera parody, "The Life and Loves of Linda Lovely," and replace them with the characters from another soap opera parody, "Mary Backstayge, Noble Wife."

From Boston, The Two and Only (yes, that's the title of their 1970 Broadway hit show) moved to New York, the center of the broadcasting universe in the 1950s. Once there, they could be heard on a bewildering variety of programs, as many as four at a time until 1976 and more occasionally after.

Mysteries were almost as fertile a field for their brand of satire as soap operas. Regular listeners might remember the men of "Squad Car 119;" that vulnerable private eye, "Blimmix"; or the code-loving secret agent, "Elmer W. Litzinger, Spy." Truly venerable listeners may know of "Mr. Keen, Tracer of Lost Persons," a real life radio show of the vintage of the real life Mary Noble, Backstage Wife, and the basis for this parody. If you find this confusing, good. That should put you in the exactly proper frame of mind for what is to follow.

* * *

(Music: Somber and mysterious)

BOB   It's mystery time on the Bob and Ray show. Presenting Mr. Treet, Chaser of Lost People. Today, the surly old investigator takes from his files the case he calls, "The Overdose of Very Fatal Poison Murder Clue."

(Music: Out)

BOB   Our story opens in the luxurious New York penthouse apartment of Wealthy Jacobus Pike, famous backer of Broadway plays. As we hear Pike call for his valet, Rudy...

PIKE   Rudy, come here!

(Door opens)

RUDY   *(Coming on)* You call, Mr. Pike?

PIKE   Yes, Rudy. I want you to take this manuscript back to Greg Marlowe, young playwright who is secretly in love with my sister, Julia, who dreams of a career on the stage. There is a note inside which explains to him my reason for refusing to back his play on Broadway.

RUDY   Okay, Mr. Pike. I'll be back as soon as possible.

(*Door closes*)

PIKE   That young upstart thinks he can coerce me into putting up my money for any such ridiculous play as that. Well, he has another—What? How did you get in here? What do you want? No, no, don't shoot me with that gun you're holding. I'll do anything. Don't come any closer. No, no.

(*Gunshots; body falls to floor*)

PIKE   Oooh. You've murdered me. You sneaked in here wearing the disguise of someone I don't know, waited until I was alone and then you killed me. (*Moaning*) I'm dead.

BOB   Several hours later in the office of Mr. Treet, Chaser of Lost People, we see the surly old investigator at his desk as his assistant Spike Glancy ushers in a tall young man with dark features. We hear Spike say...

SPIKE   This gentleman wants to see you, boss.

TREET   Usher him in, Spike.

SPIKE   He's a tall young man with dark features.

TREET   I can see that, Spike.

SPIKE   He looks guilty to me, boss.

TREET   No man is innocent if he is proven guilty, Spike. Show him in.

SPIKE   You see, mister? I told you Mr. Treet was fair.

TREET   That will be all, Spike. Sit down, sir.

SPIKE   I'll be right outside if you need me, boss.

TREET   All right.

(*Door closes*)

TREET   Now, what can I do for you, sir?

MARLOWE   Mr. Treet, I am Gregory Marlowe, young playwright secretly in love with Wealthy Jacobus Pike's
sister, Julia, who dreams of a career on the stage.

TREET   (*Interrupting*) Come, come, young man, you'll have
to put your cards on the table if you want me to help
you.

MARLOWE   I'm coming to that, Mr. Treet. This morning I
went to Pike's expensive New York penthouse
apartment...

TREET   (*Interrupting*)   You went there believing that Pike's
sister, Julia, had talked her brother, Wealthy Jacobus,
into putting up the money for the new play that you've
written.

MARLOWE   Mr. Treet, you're uncanny!

TREET   I'm right, then?

MARLOWE   No. I went there expecting to have Pike give
me a check for my play so that I can start producing it
next week.

TREET   Aha! What did you find, Marlowe?

MARLOWE   I found Pike dead, Mr. Treet.

TREET   Dead?

MARLOWE   Dead, Mr. Treet. Murdered by an overdose of a
very fatal poison.

TREET   Dreadful! And you want me...?

MARLOWE   I want you to help me, Mr. Treet.

TREET   Well, I'll do my best. My assistant Spike and you and I will first go to the murdered man's apartment. Oh, Spike?

SPIKE   Yes, boss?

TREET   Open the door before you come in.

SPIKE   Oh, I'm sorry.

(*Door opens*)

SPIKE   Yes, boss, what can I do?

TREET   Get my car out, Spike. Mr. Marlowe, here, is going to accompany us to the apartment of the late Wealthy Jacobus Pike. I think we have stumbled on a murder.

(*Music: Stab and out. Sound: Knocks on door*)

MARLOWE   I hope we are not too late, Mr. Treet.

(*Door opens*)

RUDY   Oh, it's you, Mr. Marlowe.

MARLOWE   Hello, Rudy, this is Mr. Treet, Chaser...

RUDY   Not the surly old investigator?

SPIKE   That's right, Bucko, and who might you be?

TREET   If I'm not mistaken, Spike, this is Rudy, Mr. Pike's valet.

MARLOWE   That's right, Mr. Treet.

RUDY   Oh, I've hoid a lot about you, Mr. Treet. Come in.

(*Door closes*)

MARLOWE   There he is, Mr. Chase. Over there on the floor where I found him.

TREET   The name is Treet, Marlowe.

SPIKE   He seems nervous, boss. Shall I frisk him?

TREET   No, that's not necessary, I have already seen to
that. Oh, Rudy, will you ask Julia Pike, Wealthy's
sister, to step in here, please?

SPIKE   Boss, Greg Marlowe, here, is a young playwright
secretly in love with Julia, who dreams of a career on
the stage.

TREET   Exactly, Spike. I want to question everybody.

MARLOWE   But, Mr. Treet, Julia doesn't have anything to
do with...

(*Door opens*)

TREET   Ah, Miss Julia Pike?

JULIA   You sent for me, Mr. Chase?

TREET   Yes, cóme in, Julia. Sit down.

SPIKE   And the name is Lost, Miss Pike, not Chase.

(*Door closes*)

TREET   No, Spike, you're People, and I'm Treeter chasing
lost vistas.

MARLOWE   Well, aren't you a little misted yourself, Trace?

RUDY   If you folks don't mind, I'll just step out to the
kitchen.

SPIKE   Not so fast, Rudy. Mr. Trader here thinks you lose
people.

TREET   Or at least we'll chase it that way for now.

JULIA   Mr. Loster, you have chosen a lot of treats in your
career.

TREET   On the contrary, Julia, cheating is not tracing
choosers.

SPIKE   And if anyone can lose my boss, Mr. Cheepful here can poop!

TREET   Thanks for the vote of treetle, Pete.

JULIA   I have a headache, Mr. Poet. May I chapel to the lost room and treat?

TREET   Not so fast, Julia. Spike, get my car.

SPIKE   Right, boss.

TREET   No one is to leave this room until I get back. In the meantime, you are all under suspicion. I think every one of you is lost.

(*Music: Stab and out*)

SPIKE   But, boss, you left all the suspects back there at Wealthy Jacobus Pike's famous Broadway backer's apartment...What if they try to escape?

TREET   Exactly what I'm figuring, Spike. One of those persons—Julia Pike, sister of Wealthy Jacobus Pike, Rudy, his valet, or Greg Marlowe, handsome young playwright secretly in love with Julia (who dreams of a career on the stage)—is the guilty one.

SPIKE   Then its some kind of a trap, boss?

TREET   Quiet, Spike!

SPIKE   What?

TREET   (*Whisper*) Act as if nothing has happened, Spike. I'm sure that someone is listening outside the door. I'll just walk over to the door quietly...

(*Door opens*)

SPIKE   Who is there, boss?

TREET   No one, Spike, I could have sworn—Spike, what are you doing with that gun?

SPIKE   Pointing it at you, boss.

TREET   But you can't mean that you, that you're...

SPIKE   That's right, boss, But just as soon as I rip off this mask (*effort*), you'll see that I'm not really your assistant, Spike, but I'm—

TREET   Julia Marlowe!

JULIA   Yes, Mr. Treet.

TREET   Not Mr. Treet, Julia. As soon as I rip off my mask (*effort*), you'll see that I am really—

JULIA   Rudy! Mr. Pike's valet!

RUDY   At last we are together, in love as we are with each other!

JULIA   Rudy!

RUDY   Julia!

(*Fade in theme music under*)

BOB   And so another case from the files of Mr. Treet is marked solved. Listen next time when the surly old investigator brings us "The Shanty With the Open Door on the Old Vacant Lot across the Railroad Tracks Murder Clue."

(*Music: Tag and out*)

Write If You Get Work: The Best of Bob & Ray. NY: Random House, 1975.

John Sladek

The Purloined Butter

John Sladek's name is not well known in America, partly because he spent most of his writing life in England and partly because he never seems to write more than two books in any given genre. Gothics, science fiction and mysteries have crept from his keyboard, almost every one a mordant satire on some aspect of those fields.

He's probably best known to detective fiction fans for his *Black Aura* and *Invisible Green,* two spoofs of thirties-style impossible crime novels. Connoisseurs, however, still marvel at that blackest of black comedies, *Black Alice* (written in collaboration with Thomas M. Disch under the pseudonym Thom Demijohn), in which a blonde eleven-year-old heiress and kidnap victim is disguised in plain sight by the simple expedient of dyeing her skin black.

Such a device should of course immediately remind us of Edgar Allen Poe's "Purloined Letter." And, indeed, when Sladek chose to take on a mystery writer after a long and

biting series of science fiction parodies he started with Poe.
Return now to C. Auguste Dupin and Paris in the autumn
of 18—.

* * *

AT PARIS, JUST AFTER DARK one gusty evening in the
autumn of 18—, I was enjoying the twofold luxury of
meditation and meerschaum, in company with my friend
C. Auguste Dupin, in his little back library. The door was
thrown open and admitted our old acquaintance, Monsieur G———, the Prefect of the Parisian police.

"And what, after all, is the matter on hand?" I asked.

"Why, I will tell you," replied the Prefect. "I have
received personal information, from a very high quarter,
that a certain condiment of the last importance, has been
purloined from the royal apartments. The individual who
purloined it is known. It still remains in his possession,
which can be inferred by the nature of the condiment and
the non-appearance of certain results which would at once
arise from its passing *out* of the robber's possession."

"Then," I observed, "the butter is clearly upon the
premises. As for being on his person, I suppose that is out
of the question."

"Entirely," said the Prefect. "He has been twice waylaid,
as if by footpads, and his person rigorously searched under
my own inspection."

"And his hotel?"

"Why the fact is, we took our time and searched *everywhere*. I took the whole building, room by room; devoting
the nights of a whole week to each. We examined, first, the
furniture in each apartment. We opened every possible
drawer; and I presume you know that to a properly trained
police agent, such a thing as a *secret* drawer is impossible.
We have accurate rules; the fiftieth part of a line could not
escape us. The chair cushions we probed with the long fine
needles you have seen me employ. From the tables we

removed the tops, to examine the possibility of excavated legs; likewise the bedposts."

"You did not take to pieces all the chairs?" I asked.

"Certainly not; but we did better—we examined the rungs of every chair in the house, and indeed, the jointings of every description of furniture, by the aid of a most powerful microscope. Had there been traces of recent disturbance, we should not have failed to detect it, instantly. A single grain of gimlet dust, for example, would have been as obvious as an apple."

"I presume you looked to the mirrors, between the boards and plates, and you probed the beds, as well as the curtains and carpets?"

"That of course; and when we had completed the furniture, we then examined the house itself. We scrutinized each individual square inch throughout the premises, including the two houses immediately adjoining, with the microscope, as before. The grounds were paved with brick; examination of the moss between stones by the microscope revealed no disturbances."

Dupin spoke for the first time. "I assume the hotel is at least fifty feet on a side," he said. The Prefect nodded. "And it has at least three stories, each twenty feet high. And there are at least four rooms on each floor. If you had but a week to examine a room (assuming six hours per night available), you would have to cover"—he paused, performing lightning mental calculation—"sixteen and one-fifth square inches per second. The grain of gimlet dust you spoke of must be four or five thousandths of an inch in diameter, or one-thousandth as broad as an apple. If, therefore, one of your men were to examine one 'applesworth' of visible area per second, he would require four hundred seconds, or eighteen and two-thirds minutes, to cover a square inch.

"It follows, therefore, that it must take nine hundred sixty minutes, or sixteen hours, for one man to examine

one square foot of area. A room twenty-five feet square
and twenty in height must have a total inside area of three
thousand, two hundred and fifty square feet; one man
would require a great deal of time to examine it."

"Naturally, I employed—"

"More than one man? Indeed, I have calculated that, if
your men examined these rooms as you say, you would
have required the services of *one thousand, two hundred and
thirty-eight men,* all working away with their microscopes at
the same time, in the same smallish room! And working, as
you implied, noiselessly! Come, come, my dear Prefect!"

I was astonished. The Prefect appeared absolutely thun-
derstricken. For some moments he remained speechless
and motionless, looking incredulously at my friend with
open mouth, and eyes that seemed starting from their
sockets.

"You know very well what I mean, Monsieur G———"
said Dupin.

The Prefect blushed. Then, to my utter amazement, he
reached into his pocket and drew out the butter. Dupin
satisfied himself that this butter was indeed the one in
question, then locked it away.

"You may go," he said coldly to the Prefect. This
functionary seized his hat and stick in a perfect agony of
joy, and then scrambling and struggling to the door,
rushed at length unceremoniously from the room and
from the house.

When the Prefect had gone, my friend entered into some
explanations.

The Best of John Sladek. NY: Pocket Books, 1981.

E. C. Bentley

Greedy Night

Though it's tempting to think that somewhere in history there must have been innovators named, say, Sir Fortescue Sonnet or Guiseppe Roderico de Sestina, I know of only one verse form named for a particular person. That is, of course, the Clerihew, that four-lined double couplet invented by Edmund Clerihew Bentley.

Correct, mystery buffs, that's the same E. C. Bentley who is famed in the mystery field for his three Trent novels, the first one being the classic—and ironically titled—*Trent's Last Case*.

But it was those Clerihews that secured his fame as a humorist. The first one popped out when he was but sixteen:

Sir Humphrey Davy
Abominated gravy.
He lived in the odium
Of having discovered sodium

and they poured out by the dozens ever after, both civilized and dotty in tone in truest English style.

Bentley himself was a creature of contradiction. His own son said that "his interest in contemporary literature, especially fiction, was extraordinarily meagre," but he knew enough about mystery novels not only to write them but to recreate every one of Lord Peter Wimsey's spectacular number of idiosyncrasies. And even, while we're on the subject, to write a clerihew on Lord Peter's creator:

> Miss Dorothy Sayers
> Never cared about the Himalayas.
> The height that gave her a thrill
> Was Primrose Hill.

* * *

"Yow ow ow," observed Lord Peter Wimsey opening his eyes; then, reclosing and feebly knuckling them, "Ow wow. Yah ah ow."

"Very good, my lord," his servant said, as he drew the curtains of the bedroom. "It is now twelve o'clock noon, my lord. At what hour would your lordship take breakfast?"

"Zero hour," Lord Peter snarled. "Take the nasty breakfast away, I don't want any breakfast today. Oh Lord! Bunter, why did I drink all that Corton Clos du Roi 1904 on the top of a quart of Archdeacon ale last night? I'm old enough to know better. Anyhow, my inside is."

"If I may make the suggestion, my lord, it may have been what your lordship had after coming home that is at the root of the trouble."

Wimsey sat up in bed wild-eyed. "Bunter!" he gasped. "Don't tell me I had whisky as well."

"No, my lord. That may possibly have been your lordship's intention; but I fear that what your lordship actually drank, in a moment of absent-mindedness, was a mixture of furniture-polish and Vichy water. I found the empty bottles on the floor this morning, my lord."

Wimsey sank back with a moan; then rallied himself and swallowed a little tea from the cup which Bunter had filled.

"I don't like this tea," he said peevishly. "I don't believe this is my specially grown Son-of-Heaven china."

"It is, my lord; but in some circumstances the flavour of almost anything is apt to be sensibly impaired. May I urge, my lord, that an effort should be made to eat some breakfast? It is considered to be advisable on the morning after an occasion of festivity, even if the handle of a knife has to be employed to assist the process of deglutition."

"Oh, all right." Wimsey held out his hand for the menu which Bunter produced, like a conjurer, apparently from the air. "Well, I won't eat *avoine secoueur*, anyhow. Give it to the cat."

"The cat has already tried it, my lord, during my momentary absence from the kitchen. The intelligent animal appears to be of your lordship's opinion. I would recommend a little *pâte gonfleur sur canapé*, my lord, for the present emergency."

Wimsey groaned. "I don't believe I could taste even that," he said. "Very well, I'll have a stab at it."

"Thank you, my lord." Bunter laid an armful of newspapers on the bed and withdrew. When he returned with the breakfast tray Wimsey was reading with absorbed interest. "Bunter," he said eagerly, "I see that at Sotheby's on Monday they're auctioning a thing I simply must have—the original manuscript of the Chanson de Roland, with marginal notes by Saint Louis. If I find I can't go myself, I shall want you to pop round and bid for me. That is, of course, if it's the genuine article. You could make sure of that, I suppose?"

"Without difficulty, my lord. I have always taken an interest in the technical study of mediaeval calligraphy. I should be sceptical, though, about those marginal notes, my lord. It has always been understood, your lordship will recollect, that His Most Christian Majesty was unable to write. However—"

At this point there came a long-continued ringing at the door-bell of the flat; and after a brief interval Bunter, with all the appearance of acting under protest, showed the Bishop of Glastonbury into the bedroom.

"I say, Peter, there's the devil to pay!" exclaimed that prelate. "Topsy's pretty well off her onion, and Bill Mixer's in a frightful dither. Have you heard what's happened? But, of course, you couldn't. They've been trying to get you on the 'phone this morning, but that man of yours kept on saying that he feared his lordship was somewhat closely engaged at the moment. So they rang me up and asked me to tell you."

"Well, why not tell me?" Wimsey snapped. Topsy, the Bishop's favourite sister, was an old friend, and her husband was a man for whom Wimsey had a deep regard that dated from his years at Balliol.

"Dermot's dead."

"I say! What a ghastly thing!" Wimsey scrambled out of bed and into a dressing-gown. "What happened to poor old Dermot?"

"That's just what they don't know. There was absolutely nothing the matter with him, but he was found dead this morning—apparently uninjured, they say. Foul play is suspected, of course."

"Of course," Wimsey agreed, plying his hairbrushes vigorously.

"And Topsy and Bill would like you, if you can, to go down for the week-end—"

"Up," Wimsey murmured.

"All right, up for the week-end," said the Bishop a little testily. "And see what you can do to clear the mystery up, or down, or any dashed way you like."

Wimsey rang the bell, and Bunter instantly appeared. "Oh, look here, Bunter, will you get the German Ambassador on the 'phone for me?" As Bunter busied himself with the instrument by the bedside, Wimsey turned to the Bishop again. "Well, Mike, I will certainly go if they want me. I shall drive there in the Fendlair, so it won't take long."

The Bishop repressed a shudder. "Why do you amateur detectives always drive like bloody lunatics?" he asked plaintively. "You all do—except Trent, of course; he never does anything off-colour. Well, they'll be glad of your help—if you get there in one piece, that is—and I'm grateful to you myself. I must push off now—got to move the second reading of the Disestablishment Bill in the Lords this afternoon, and I haven't prepared a line of my stuff yet."

As the Bishop disappeared, Bunter presented the telephone receiver to Wimsey on a salver. "His Excellency is now at the apparatus, my lord."

"Hullo, is that Bodo?" Wimsey cried. "Yes, Peter speaking. Heil Hitler. I say, old man, I'm frightfully sorry, but I can't turn up at your squash this evening. I've just heard some very sad news....No, Heil Hitler, it's nobody you know.... Yes, Heil Hitler, very serious. I mean, dead, and all that. I've got to go and see about it....That's kind of you, Bodo. You know I value your sympathy. Thanks hunderttausendmal. Well, Heil Hitler, good-bye."

During the progress of his toilet, Wimsey cancelled by telephone, with all apologies due, several other appointments. A Sunday luncheon of the Food and Wine Society at Tewkesbury, to test the quality—so praised by Falstaff—of the local mustard. A meeting of the Committee of the Anerithmon Gelasma Yacht Club, called for the purpose of blackballing the Duke of Cheshire. A supper for Miss Ruth Draper, who would give, it was hoped, her impersonation of the Nine Muses discussing the character of Aphrodite.

Wimsey then got into communication with the Spoopendyke Professor of Egyptology in the University of Oxford,
and accepted in brief but sympathetic terms his invitation
to spend the weekend. Professor Mixer was greatly re-
lieved, he said. He feared that Wimsey must have sacrificed other engagements in order to do Topsy and himself
this kindness.

Wimsey burdened his soul with the statement that he
had been going to spend the next few days in bringing the
catalogue of his library up to date; a thing which could be
done at any time.

The Professor of Egyptology met Wimsey at the door of
his grey old house of Headington stone, nearly facing the
main gateway of Janus. He greeted his visitor with sub-
dued cordiality, his left hand clutching his unkempt beard
as he talked.

"It's very good of you to come, Peter," he said. "Topsy
was anxious to have your opinion, and we are very glad to
have you with us anyhow. But whatever you may find out
about the cause of death, you can't bring back poor
Dermot. I thought it better you should stay in college, if
you don't mind. This is a house of sorrow, you see; and you
would really be more comfortable in Janus. I've got you
rooms in the Fellows' Quad—Simpson's—he is in the
Morea just now. You only want to be careful not to disturb
the manuscript of his forthcoming book on the pre-
Minoan cultures of the Dodecanese. He has a habit of
doing all his writing on the backs of old envelopes, and
leaving them all over the floor. So perhaps you'd better not
use the study—you might prefer not to in any case,
because of course it can't ever be dusted on account of the
envelopes—hasn't been for years."

"I shall love staying in Janus," said Wimsey. "It's a
college I was very seldom in when I was up, and the only
experience I had of the Fellows' Quad was when Jinks was

Proctor, and I had to go to his rooms there to see him about my chaining a gorilla to the railings of the Martyrs' Memorial."

"Ha! H'm! Just so," said the Professor. "Perhaps you would like to see the body at once. It is still here, lying just as it was found—in the library."

"Well, naturally," Wimsey said with a touch of impatience. "Where did you think I thought it was?—in the scullery? Yes, I should like to see it now."

The Professor led the way to the library, a large, light room on the ground floor, walled with crowded shelves, and smelling slightly of mummied cats. Before the central window was a large writing-table covered with piles of papers in orderly array. On the blotter, Wimsey noted with interest, a very modern book lay open with a part of one of its leaves torn away—a detective story which had murdered sleep for countless readers.

The body lay on the carpet beside the table. Wimsey, mastering the emotion that seized him, knelt down and looked closely at the stocky, well-knit figure, still carefully neat in appearance as Dermot always was in life, and in a natural posture, but that the feet were somewhat drawn up. Those keen eyes were closed now, the mouth too was shut, and there was not a trace of expression on the small, aquiline features. No blood was to be seen, and there was, as Wimsey soon ascertained, no sign of any wound on the body.

Dermot had been in perfect health and excellent spirits up to the time of his death, Professor Mixer said. He himself had been the last to see him alive—at about half-past nine o'clock that morning, when they had exchanged a few words in this same room before the Professor went out to Blackwell's in quest of a book. Shortly after that his wife, passing the door of the library, had heard Dermot swearing violently within, but she had thought nothing of that.

"You remember, Peter," the Professor said, "how rough

his language often was. He picked up the habit during his time in the mercantile marine, and he seemed quite unable to break himself of it. Topsy, you know, rather admired it really, and I never paid any attention to it; but it cost us the services of an excellent cook, a strict Wesleyan, and sometimes I felt rather uncomfortable about it when I was seeing pupils here."

"Do you think he could have taught them anything?" Wimsey asked.

"I fear so—yes. I mean, I hope so," said the Professor with a melancholy shake of the head. "Only last week Lord Torquilstone brought me an essay, and as soon as he entered the room Dermot called out—well, I cannot bring myself to repeat what he said. It was as essentially meaningless as it was deplorably coarse, and Torquilstone was quite taken aback. Then there was another time, when the Vice-Chancellor came to tea with us. We were in the drawing-room upstairs, but I am afraid that he distinctly heard Dermot, who was in this room, blaspheming in the most dreadful terms. In fact, Hoggarty must have heard, because he dropped a piece of muffin into his tea, and then remarked upon the lovely weather that we were having—which was not the case, for it was pouring with rain and very cold for the time of the year. I fear I shall be getting quite a bad name in the Hebdomadal Council."

"And was that—I mean what Topsy heard—the last evidence of his being alive?"

"Yes. It is painful," the Professor said, "to think that those were in all probability his last words; for I came in about half an hour later, and found him as you see."

Dinner with Professor Mixer and his wife that evening was not a cheerful affair. Topsy, pale and red-eyed, strangled a sob from time to time, and made hardly a pretence of eating. Her husband, too, could do no more than peck feebly at a half-raw cutlet, while his talk (about the funerary customs which grew up under the Kyksos dynasty) had little of its customary sparkle.

Wimsey, on the other hand, urged on by some impulse which he could neither understand nor control, ate enough of the repulsive meal for all three, while yet he shuddered to think of the probable consequences. He sketched in fancy a lyrical dialogue between himself and his digestion:

"Know'st thou not me?" the deep voice cried.
"So long enjoyed, so oft misused;
"Alternate, in thy fickle pride,
"Extolled, neglected and accused..."

At length he took himself away, and retired to his sitting-room in college to think over all that he had learned from the Professor before dinner-time, and from his interrogation of Topsy and the servants. The case baffled him.

He sat at his window on the first floor, looking out, in the gathering gloom, upon the velvet lawn and the stately background of fifteenth-century architecture, pierced just opposite his place of observation by a broad, low-pointed archway through which a section of the Front Quad could be faintly discerned. The Aquinas Club, he had been told, were holding their annual dinner that night, by invitation of the Fellows, in the Senior Common Room, and for some time past their proceedings, which were fully choral, had claimed his attention. He heard the tremendous burden of "On Ilkley Moor Baat 'At," the stirring swing of "Auprès de la Blonde," the complex cadences of "Green Grow the Rashes Oh!" the noble organ-music of "Slattery's Mounted Foot," the crashing staccato of "Still His Whiskers Grew," the solemn keening of "The Typist's Farewell." Once there were indications that a Rhodes Scholar was trying, with as little success as usually waits on his countrymen's efforts in that direction, to remember the words of his own national anthem.

Then there fell a hush; and it was not until half an hour later that Wimsey's wrestling with his problem was disturbed by new sounds of academic liveliness in the Front Quad. He gazed expectantly towards the great archway, and presently a slight, pyjamaed figure fled across the darksome frame of vision, pursued by a loose group of obscurer shapes, dimly seen to be white-shirted, and quite plainly heard to yell. Wimsey sighed. The luxurious, self-conscious melancholy of those no longer ridiculously young, but having—with any luck—half a lifetime still before them, possessed him. Elbows on sill, chin in hands, he gazed into the now untenanted gloom, recalling lost binges of old years.

A little later the moon peered out from her curtains of cloud, and Wimsey, finding that his mood demanded some further recapturing of the spirit of a college by night, descended into the Quad and set out on a voyage of discovery. In the wall to his left hand an opening that looked like the doorway to a staircase of rooms, such as he had just quitted, turned out to be the archway of a vaulted passage leading into a tiny square of stone, whose small grated windows and peaked turret recalled one of Doré's visions of the Paris of Rabelais. From this another entry led to another Quad, of normal size, and thence again he passed to one yet larger, which he could recognise by the battlements on the further wall, the outer wall of Janus, as Pateshull Quad.

As Wimsey stood at gaze, imagining what study, what talk, or possibly what *chemin-de-fer,* might be in progress behind the few windows that still showed lights within, a young man emerged from one of the staircase entries. He was white-shirted, his hair was somewhat disordered, and he carried under one arm an enormous book. This he took to the centre of the gravelled space, then placed it carefully on the ground, and sat upon it. Soon his wandering eye caught sight of Wimsey in the moonlight, and the two inspected one another in silence for some moments. Then the keen instinct of youth told the sitter that the figure before him, slender though it was, must be that of someone of thirty at least, and with instant deference to age and infirmity he rose and waved a hand towards the obese volume on the gravel.

"Won't you sit down, sir?" he said. "Not enough room for two, I'm afraid, even on Liddell and Scott."

"Thanks, I'd rather not," Wimsey said. "I'm staying in your Fellows' Quad, and I just came out for a stroll before turning in. You have been at the Aquinas dinner, perhaps?"

"Yes," said the young man. "It was rather progressive, as a dinner—sort of thing makes you feel a trifle listless afterwards—so, if you're sure you won't—" He subsided upon his lexicon, then went on: "Young Warlock got it up his nose rather, you see, and went to sleep on the sofa, so we carried him to his rooms and put him to bed. Then the little devil woke up suddenly and got loose, and we had to chase him all over the college before we could get him bedded down again. Now I'm just sitting here for rest and meditation. D'you ever meditate?"

"Oh, often," said Wimsey. "What were you thinking of meditating upon this time?"

"Housman's edition of Manilius," the young man an swered, abstractedly removing his collar and tie. "Wonderful chap—Housman, I mean; Manilius was rather a blister. The way Housman pastes the other commentators in the slats does your heart good. I was just concentrating on the way he kicks the stuffing out of Elias Stöber—lovely!"

"Well, I won't interrupt you," Wimsey said. "I'm thinking something over myself, as a matter of fact."

"All right, go to it," the young man said amiably; then,

lifting up his voice in an agreeable baritone, "I never envy a-a-anyone when I'm thinking…thinking…thinking…. I say," he added, "who are you? I'm Mitchell, named Bryan Farrant by my innocent parents; so of course I'm never called anything but B.F."

"Hard luck! My name's Wimsey."

"Not Lord Peter?"

"Yes."

"Sinful Solomon!" exclaimed the young man. "Here, you simply must confer distinction on my lexicon. I'll have the cover you sat on framed."

"No, really," Wimsey laughed, "I must go. But do you and your friends really read the chronicles of my misspent life, then?"

"Do we read them?" cried Mr. Mitchell. "I should say we do read them! We eat them!"

"How jolly for you—I mean for me—that is to say, for her—oh well, you know what I mean," Wimsey said distractedly.

"I suppose I do, if you say so," said Mr. Mitchell without conviction. "You know the lyric there is about you?

> *Lord Peter Wimsey*
> *May look a little flimsy,*
> *But he's simply sublime*
> *When nosing out a crime.*"

"No, I hadn't heard it," Wimsey said. "It's nice to be sublime, anyhow. Well, here I go. Good night."

"Sweet dreams!" said Mr. Mitchell.

On the Sunday morning Wimsey awoke with that indescribable feeling that something has happened, but one does not know quite what. Mr. Mitchell's parting wish had been not too exactly fulfilled. Wimsey had dreamed of having his head bitten off by a crocodile, after which he had attended a Yorkshire farmers' market-day ordinary, and then, in the character of a missionary, had been chased by a cassowary over the plains of Timbuctoo.

He arose unrefreshed. From his bedroom window he perceived a College servant approaching the entrance to his staircase. The hour being no later than seven o'clock, the scout, who was in his shirtsleeves, had a broom over his left shoulder, a teapot in his right hand, an old cap on back to front, and a cigarette behind one of his ears. He was eating.

"What would Bunter say? Perish Bunter!" mused Wimsey ungratefully. "I am in the arms of Alma Mater once more, and this—this is one of the conditions of her kindness. I wonder what that scout is eating. I never saw Bunter eat. Perhaps he never does—it's a low habit, eating."

Eating! The term recurred again and again to Wimsey's mind as he prepared himself for the facing of another day. What was it that was trying to force itself into the realm of consciousness?

An hour later, the scout, looking now much less like a hangman's assistant, set out for him that Oxford breakfast whose origin is not to be descried through the mist of ages—coffee, scrambled eggs and bacon, toast, butter, marmalade. "And a jolly good breakfast too!" Wimsey reflected. "What was good enough for Duns Scotus and St. Edmund, Roger Bacon and More, Erasmus and Bodley, is good enough for me. And in this holy city I seem always to be hungry. How I always eat at Oxford!"

There again! Back came his mind to eating, though all the year round he would breakfast without a moment's thought for the alimentary process.

Suddenly Wimsey thrust back his chair from the table. "My dream!" he cried hoarsely, striking his forehead with his hand, which at the moment was holding a spoon filled with marmalade. "Eating! That was the concept which the Unknown I was pushing at the Conscious Me! What did young B.F. say? They eat them!"

Wimsey dashed impetuously from the room.

Scene: The library at the Spoopendyke Professor's house. Present: Topsy, her husband, Lord Peter Wimsey and the corpse. Armed with a letter-opener taken from the writing-table, Wimsey knelt beside all that was mortal of Dermot, and gently prised apart the firm-set jaws. From the open mouth he drew forth a piece of printed paper, and smoothed it out upon the table-top beside the novel that still lay there, open at a page of which a part had been torn away. In silence he fitted the scrap into its place in the mutilated page, then pointed to the title at its head.

"*Strong Poison!*"[1] he said in a low voice. "Too strong indeed for poor Dermot. Such is the magic of that incisive, compelling style that even the very printed word is saturated with the essence of what it imparts. Others eat her works in a figurative sense only; Dermot began to eat this one in truth and in fact, and so rushed, all unknowing, on his doom."

Topsy burst into tears. "Uh! Uh! Uh!" she said. "Why did you leave the bub-bub-book about, Bill? You knew he never could, uh! uh! resist an open book."

"But how was I to know the story was such a powerful one?" the Professor groaned. "I am no judge of any literature later than 1300 B.C."

Wimsey stood with bowed head. "You have one small consolation," he said, laying a hand on Topsy's shoulder. "Death must have been instantaneous. Dear old Dermot!" he mused. "He was a priceless old bird."

---

[1] Dorothy L. Sayers (Gollancz, 1930).

"Well, not exactly priceless," the Professor said with academic care for the niceties of expression. "Topsy bought him in Caledonian Market for three pounds, including the cage."

"You ought to have put him bub-bub-back in it when you went out," Topsy sobbed.

"I know. I shall never forgive myself," said the Professor dismally. "I did think of it, in fact, but when I suggested it Dermot cursed me so frightfully that I left him at liberty."

"He was chu-chu-cheap at the money," Topsy howled. "When once I had heard him sus-sus-swear I would have gone to a fuf-fuf-fiver. I had never heard anything lul-lul-like it."

"No! Hadn't you though?" Wimsey was interested. "And you were at Somerville, too."

Parody Party. Ed. by Leonard Russell. London: Hutchinson, 1936.

Fran Lebowitz

In Hot Pursuit

Fran Lebowitz is a curmudgeon's curmudgeon. A complete listing of those things she actually approves of can probably be inscribed on a fingernail, although she takes a perverse, voluble, and perpetually hoarse delight in staunchly defending her three-pack-a-day cigarette habit.

If that's a bit out of fashion, so be it. She has taken great pride in not fitting in since getting kicked out of a fashionable private school in her senior year. She eventually obtained a high school equivalency diploma but never bothered with college, about which she sees no value, having mastered the English language pretty well on her own.

It is impossible to imagine her living anywhere else than in New York City, if only because the city offers more to kvetch about per square inch than anywhere else in the world. Lebowitz has fulminated against plants, people who serve apple juice with dinner, wall-to-wall carpeting in bathrooms, women who wear athletic shoes with suits, brown rice, and guilt. She was a New York cult figure writing for an audience of "forty decorators" in Andy Warhol's *Interview* (and later *Mademoiselle*) when her collection *Metropolitan Life* became a surprise best seller in 1978. *Social Studies* followed in 1981, then silence. She claims the reason is simple. A meticulous writer who "polishes her sentences to an aphoristic sharpness," as one critic put it, she now insists upon a clause in any contract forbidding any editor to change a word of her prose. Editors, being the creatures they are, for the most part stopped publishing her. A novel, tentatively titled *Exterior Signs of Wealth*, has long been rumored. Since one of the few things Lebowitz does approve of is procrastination, one would do well to look forward to it without holding one's breath.

As might be expected, Lebowitz's take on Sherlock Holmes is decidedly off center. There is not another Holmesian parody to be found that comes close to the case Lebowitz refers to as "A Study in Harlots."

* * *

THERE RECENTLY APPEARED in the *New York Post* an article concerning the sexual abuse and exploitation of several thousand young boys in the Los Angeles area. Hard facts were on the sparse side but the police department did make some estimates.

More than 3,000 children under the age of fourteen are being exploited sexually in the Los Angeles area.

At least 2,000 local adult males actively pursue boys under the age of fourteen.

More than 25,000 juveniles from fourteen to seventeen years of age are used sexually by approximately 15,000 adult males.

I was, of course, surprised to see so many numbers on a list of what were admittedly allegations and wondered just where they had gotten their figures. It was difficult to imagine the police actually going around counting, so instead I imagined this:

A Study in Harlots

In thinking back on the many exhilarating and arduous adventures that I have shared with my friend Mr. Sherlock Homes and Gardens, I can recall none more perplexing (or more fun) than that which I have chosen to call *A Study in Harlots*. Of course, *The Case of Dom Pérignon 1966* presented its problems, *The Afghan Hound of the Baskervilles* was hardly easy and *The Baker Street Extremely Irregulars* was no piece of chicken, but none was a match for the tale I now tell.

First, allow me to introduce myself. I am Dr. John Watson, although Homes and Gardens often refers to me simply as "my dear." I am a qualified physician with a limited practice in the East Sixties (right near Halston's) and, I must say, much in demand, for between my own work and my association with Homes and Gardens it is generally acknowledged that Dr. John Watson knows exactly where all the bodies are buried. Homes and Gardens and I dwelt, of course, for many years at 221-B Baker Street, but the plummeting pound and outrageous taxes drove us from London, just as it did Mick, Liz, and so many other of our friends. We have taken up residence in Manhattan at an excellent address between Park and Madison (right near Halston's) and it is here that our story begins.

It was approximately eleven o'clock on a pleasant morning in early December when I descended the staircase of our tastefully appointed duplex penthouse. Homes and

Gardens, an earlier riser than I, had already breakfasted and was lying, eyes closed, on the damask-covered Empire Récamier. Edward, a very attractive young man whose acquaintance we had recently made, played Homes and Garden's violin for him. Homes and Gardens used, of course, to play his own violin, but that was before we made it. Homes and Gardens stretched a languid hand in greeting, his well-cut silk Saint Laurent shirtsleeve in graceful folds around his wrist, and said, "Watson, my dear, I see that you are a bit weary after your long evening in which you first attended a cocktail party in honor of Bill Blass's new sheet collection, had dinner at Pearl's with a number of fashion notables, drank brandy at Elaine's with a well-known author, danced at Regine's with a famous person's daughter, and then went downtown to do it with a stranger." I fell into a Louis XVI Marquise and looked at Homes and Gardens wonderingly, for all my years of being roommates with him had done nothing to diminish my astonishment at his remarkable powers of deduction. "How did you know?" I asked as soon as I had regained my composure. "I didn't see you at all yesterday, for you were busy being photographed for *L'Uomo Vogue* and I had no chance to tell you of my plans." "Elementary, my dear: The first four items I observed this morning in *Women's Wear Daily*, the last I deduced by noting that your indigo blue Jackie Rogers jacket is lying more smoothly than usual against your seriously white Vivella sweater, indicating that your somewhat recherché Fendi wallet is missing." My hand flew to my inside breast pocket but I knew it was futile, for Homes and Gardens was never wrong. "There, there, Watson my dear, no use getting into a snit about it— your wallet for a moment's pleasure is a rough trade, to be sure, but I think I have something that will take your mind off your loss. This morning there was a message on the service from Precious Little asking that we take the next flight to Los Angeles, as my assistance is required in a matter of no small delicacy."

Precious Little was an interesting fellow, though rather given to ancestor worship (other people's ancestors—he had none of his own to speak of) and Homes and Gardens had known him for years. His association with the Los Angeles Police Department was not exactly professional. He was not an officer of the law or even really a crime buff—it was, to be perfectly frank, quite simply that he had a most singular fondness for uniforms. Whatever his shortcomings, Precious was on the right side of the law and Homes and Gardens had aided him previously.

"Have our bags packed, my dear," said Homes and Gardens as he reached for the cocaine bottle, "I'll just do a few lines and then we must depart immediately." I made all haste and soon found myself sitting comfortably in the first-class compartment of a 747. A young woman in an ill-fitting pantsuit came to take our drink order. Homes and Gardens looked at her keenly yet disdainfuly and said, "Stolichnaya straight up—for I can see that you had a difficult time of it, what with the five whiskey sours you consumed before finally meeting that account executive, and the poor-quality but large quantity of marijuana that you smoked with the sales manager you ran into this morning when leaving the account executive's apartment in the East Seventies near Third Avenue." The young woman gasped in disbelief and stuttered, "But, sir—how did you—how did you...?"

"Elementary," he said coolly, "all stewardesses are alike."

I chuckled appreciatively, Homes and Gardens turned to me and said, "Now, my dear, I will tell you all that Precious told me, so that you are prepared to observe me observing the situation. It seems that a certain captain in the Los Angeles Police Department, you know who I mean, has been giving estimates to the press about the number of people involved in an underage homosexual sex scandal. Precious feels (and not without reason) that the situation is being exaggerated—you know how our captain brags— and I have been asked to investigate the matter more thoroughly, for my way with a number is legend." "Yes indeed," I agreed, "they've certainly chosen the right man." Homes and Gardens lit his pipe and I sat back with a magazine. The rest of the flight was uneventful except for a slight altercation caused by some passengers who resented Homes and Gardens telling them how the movie ended before it even started ("Saw it at a screening last week," he confided to me triumphantly), but it was all soon settled and we arrived on schedule.

Precious Little had sent his matching car and driver and the ride to the hotel was a pleasant one. The Beverly Hills has in recent years lost a bit of its cachet, but Homes and Gardens is rather attached to its paging system and I myself am partial to its distinctive pink note-pads.

No sooner had we settled into our bungalow (rather far from Halston's but right near the main building) than Precious himself arrived. "My Sher, my dear," he greeted us effusively and kissed us each on both cheeks, "you must come with me at once. That captain is becoming absolutely impossible. Daily his figures become more ridiculous and I have it from a very good source that he's hours away from talking to Rona."

"Well, well, Precious," said Homes and Garden crisply, "that, of course, must be prevented, although it is unlikely, don't you think, that she'll take his call?" We all agreed and once more I was struck by Homes and Gardens's acute sensibilities.

The three of us got into the car—Homes and Gardens electing to sit up front, in order, he said, that he might see more clearly, although I imagine that what he wanted to see more clearly did not entirely exclude Juan, Precious's superbly café-au-lait driver. Homes and Gardens is, after all, a man of many interests.

We made an extensive tour of the various neighborhoods—Homes and Gardens gazing intently at every detail while Precious pointed out the homes of the stars. Our inspection completed, we repaired to·Mr. Chow's, where we were welcomed extravagantly.

Precious and I looked at Homes and Gardens expectantly, but he avoided our eyes and I must confess that my heart sank as I allowed myself to feel for the very first time some doubt about my roommate. My spirits rose, however, when Homes and Gardens smiled precisely and said, "Oh, look, there's Liza, doesn't she look great?" I turned around and was pleased to see the celebrated entertainer waving cheerfully in our direction. We exchanged nods and turned our attention once again to Homes and Gardens, who was now obviously ready to address us.

"It's quite a simple thing really, reminds me in fact of the case involving the disappearance of a makeup artist at the *pret-à porter* some years back. We knew for a fact that a makeup artist was missing—what we didn't know was just which makeup artist it was. Everyone, as you can imagine, was in a veritable tizzy, until I pointed out that we had only to examine the faces of the models, note which ones were most painfully lacking in cheekbone definition, inquire as to who did the makeup and thus we would have the name of the missing artist. From there the actual discovery of the young man took but a moment. Now, in the instance at hand, I must say we were most fortunate that the areas involved were not the very best, for had we been concerned with, say, an area like Bel Air, we would have been confronted with the problem of ample household help. Since, however, we were dealing with such locales as Brentwood my work was quite trifling. You may have noticed, my dears, that I took much interest in the landscaping and I found exactly what I thought I would. A great many of the lawns were overgrown and needed cutting in the most dreadful way. I further learned that in many of the houses the garbage had not been taken out for days, nor had newspapers been delivered in quite some time. So many chores and part-time jobs left undone pointed to one thing and one thing only—that these neighborhoods were suffering from a dearth of underage boys. I simply counted up the amount of neglected work and can now present you with an accurate tally:

1,582 children under the age of fourteen are being exploited sexually in the Los Angeles area. 1,584, to be exact, but the other two are movie stars, which is, I regret, not illegal.

At least 10,000 local adult males actively pursue boys under the age of fourteen, but only 1,183 actually catch them.

8,000 juveniles from fourteen to seventeen years of age are used sexually by approximately 14,000 adult males (rather slim pickings, that) but 28,561 adult males are used to far greater advantage by 19,500 very crafty juveniles, many claiming to be from fourteen to seventeen years of age.

Homes and Gardens sat back with a satisfied air and Precious Little and I congratulated him heartily. Once again Homes and Garden's admirable talents had triumphed, and on the way way out of the restaurant we saw Barbra and Jon snubbing Kris.

Fran Lebowitz. *Metropolitan Life*. A Henry Robbins Book, E.P. Dutton, New York.
© 1974, 1975, 1976, 1977, 1978.

P. G. Wodehouse

About These Mystery Stories

And so, tidily, we end with Pelham Grenville Wodehouse, and not just because he's last in alphabetical order. (From Allen to Wodehouse: it would have been a temptation too great to pass up if it hadn't come about, I swear, accidentally.)

Mystery writers are known for being prolific writers of light entertainment, but all but a few must take a back seat to Wodehouse. Twenty years before his death, a mere fifty years into his writing career, he commented that he had written "ten books for boys, one book for children, forty-three novels, three hundred and fifteen short stories, four hundred and eleven articles, and a thing called *The Swoop*," not to mention being "author or co-author of sixteen plays and twenty-two musical comedies." His stories about Bertie Wooster, upper-class twit, and Jeeves, that most efficacious of valets, are undoubtedly the most famous, and are sure to stay that way—helped along by the recent series on PBS, which captured every nuance of the duo—but one mustn't forget such other series characters as Mr. Mulliner, Psmith, Ukridge, Lord Emsworth, and the magnificently named Freddie· Threepwood.

One doesn't expect parody from Wodehouse, who was too wedded to his own easily parodied style, and one doesn't get it either. And yet, paradoxically, parody there is in this essay *on* the mystery, because there is no other way to present those classic stereotypes of the mystery's 1920's Golden Age: The Sleuth with a Smile, the Moronic Master Criminal, and the One Satisfactory Villain. "One scarcely knows whether to laugh or weep," Wodehouse says of them in this article originally published in 1929. But we know, and we continue to laugh, just as we have for the past sixty-odd years.

* * *

IT IS AN ODD FACT, frequently commented upon by thoughtful observers, that most of the great plagues in history have crept on the world insidiously and without warning. Nobody notices that anything in particular is happening, until one day the populace wakes up to find the trouble full-blown in its midst.

In the Middle Ages, for instance, everything was perfectly peaceful and normal—knights jousting, swineherds tending pigs, landowners busy with soc and seizin and all that sort of thing—when one morning—on a Tuesday it was, six weeks come Lammas Eve—a varlet, strolling along the road between Southampton and Winchester—where the filling station is now—encountered a malapert knave and fell into conversation with him after the sociable fashion of those days.

"How now?" quoth the varlet.

"Ye same to you," said the knave courteously.

After which, as usually happens when two sons of the soil get together for a chat, there was a pause of about twenty minutes. At the end of this period the varlet spoke. "In my village there hath chanced a happening," he said, "which hath caused much marvel. Rummy, is ye general verdict. Old Bill of ye Mill suddenly turned black yesterday."

"Black?" said the knave, wondering.

"Black is right."

"Well, by St. James of Compostella, if this doth not beat ye band!" exclaimed the knave. "Down where I live, George ye Cowherd hath turned black too."

"Thou dost not say!"

"Of a verity I do say."

"What can have caused this?" cried the varlet.

"I could not tell thee," said the knave. "I am a stranger in these parts myself."

And a week later the Black Death was all over the country, and a man who did not look like Al Jolson singing "Sonny Boy" could scarcely be found anywhere.

ADVICE TO MY SON JOHN

IN MUCH the same way, quietly and, as it were, surreptitiously, the present flood of mystery stories has engulfed the British Isles. Only a short time ago the evil appeared merely sporadic. Now we are up to our necks in the things, and more coming all the time. There seems to be some virus in the human system just now which causes the best writers to turn out thrillers. This would not matter so much, only, unfortunately, it causes the worst of writers to turn them out too. The result is that this royal throne of kings, this sceptered isle, this earth of majesty, this seat of Mars, this other Eden, demiparadise, this fortress built by Nature for herself against infection and the hand of war, this happy breed of men, this little world, this precious stone set in the silver sea, which serves it in the office of a wall or as a moat defensive of a house—I need scarcely say that I allude to England—has degenerated into an asylum full of goofs reading one another's detective stories. And ninety-nine out of every hundred a dud.

A disquieting thought.

It does not seem to occur to the ordinary man how hard it is to do this sort of thing well. If I had a son who was thinking of writing mystery stories—and if I had a son of an age to hold a pen, that is certainly what he would be doing nowadays—I should take him aside and try to point out some of the difficulties lying in his path.

"James—or John—" I should say, "think well! Never forget that over every mystery story there broods the shadow of a yawning reader saying 'What of it?' You tell him that Sir Gregory Bulstrode has been found murdered in his library. 'Who cares?' is his reply. You add that all the doors and windows were locked. 'They always are,' he says. 'And suspicion points to at least half a dozen people!' you scream. 'Oh, well,' he mumbles, dozing off, 'it turns out in the end that one of them did it, I suppose?'"

That is the trouble. For the mystery novel Suspicion Handicap, the field is limited. You know it wasn't the hero or the heroine who did the murder. You are practically sure it couldn't have been Reggie Banks, because he is a comic character, and any vestige of humor in any character in a mystery story automatically rules him out as a potential criminal. It can't have been Uncle Joe, because he is explicitly stated to be kind to dogs. So you assume it must have been some totally uninteresting minor character who hardly ever appears and who is disclosed on the last page as the son of the inventor whom the murdered man swindled forty years ago. At any rate, you know quite well it's one of them.

WHO KILLED SIR RALPH?

IF I WERE writing a mystery story I would go boldly out for the big sensation. I would not have the crime committed by anybody in the book at all. Here are the last few paragraphs of a little thing I could write in a couple of weeks if I had not a soul above this form of literature:

"You say, Jerningham," I gasped, "that you have solved this inscrutable problem? You really know who it was that stabbed Sir Ralph with the Oriental paper knife?"

Travers Jerningham nodded curtly. I was astonished to see that he displayed none of that satisfaction which one would naturally have expected.

"I do," he said.

"But you seem gloomy, Jerningham—moody. Why is this?"

"Because it is impossible to bring the criminals to justice."

"Criminals? Was there more than one?"

"There were two, Woodger. Two of the blackest-hearted menaces to society that ever clutched a knife handle. One held Sir Ralph down, the other did the stabbing."

"But if you are so sure of this, how is it, Jerningham, that you cannot give the scoundrels their just deserts?"

Travers Jerningham laughed a bitter laugh.

"Because, Woodger, they aren't in the book at all. The fiends were too cunning to let themselves get beyond the title page. The murderers of Sir Ralph Rackstraw were Messrs. Hodder and Stoughton."

THE END

That would be something like a punch. And it is punch that the average detective story lacks.

It will be noted that in the above I have stuck to what I

might call the Gents' Ordinary or Stock-Size detectives. Travers Jerningham, if he ever comes to fruition—if "fruition" is the word I want; a thing of which I am by no means sure—will be just one more of those curt, hawk-faced, amateur investigators. It is not merely that I cannot be bothered to vary the type; I feel that, if you are going to have an amateur investigator, this even now is still the best sort to employ.

The alternatives are, of course:

(*a*) The Dry,

(*b*) The Dull,

(*c*) The Effervescent;

and I am not very fond of any of them.

The Dry Detective is elderly. He wears pince-nez and a funny hat, and is apt to cough primly. He is fussy and old-maidish. He comes within an ace of doddering. Of course, get him in a corner and he suddenly produces a punch like a prize fighter, but out of his corner he is rather a bore.

Not such a bore, of course, as the Dull Detective. This is the one who unmasks criminals by means of his special knowledge of toxics and things, and gets on the villain's track owing to the discovery that the latter is definitely brachycephalic. This is a pest.

The Effervescent Detective is rather a new invention. He is a bright young fellow of independent means whose hobby is the solution of problems. They like him at Scotland Yard, and he chaffs them. Sometimes Inspector Faraday is a little inclined to shake his head at the young man's suggestions, but he is the first to admit that Tony Dalrymple has an uncanny knack of being right. And the dear chap is so delightfully flippant with it all. None of that "Holmes, who has done this fearful thing?" stuff about him. Violence to the person cannot damp Tony's spirits, provided it is to some other person. Viewing the body brings out all that is gayest and sprightliest in him.

THE SLEUTH WITH A SMILE

"So THIS is the jolly old corpse, is it, inspector? Well, well, well! Bean bashed in and a bit of no-good done to the merry old jugular, what? Tut, tut, mother won't like this at all. You're on to the fact that the merchant who messed this cove up was left-handed and parted his hair in the middle, of course? And a good job he made of it, didn't he?"

Not a frightfully attractive young man. But spreading, I regret to say. You meet him everywhere nowadays.

The best detectives—Edgar Wallace's—are always Scotland Yard men. To a public surfeited with brilliant amateurs there is something very restful about the man from Scotland Yard. He has a background. You can believe in him. If I found it impossible to head my son off from writing mystery stories, I should advise him to give his heroes an official standing. Then he would have the Record and Finger-Print Department at his back and, if he wanted to stop the villain leaving London, he could tell off three thousand policemen to watch the roads.

It is true that the villain would get through just the same, but you can't say it isn't nice to have the sympathy and moral support of three thousand policemen.

I have got James—or John, as the case may be—pretty clear, then, on the detective end of the job. He has now to face a far more serious problem. What of the villain?

THE MORONIC MASTER CRIMINAL

VILLAINS in mystery stories may be divided broadly into three classes—all silly.

(*a*) Sinister men from China or Assam or Java or India or Tibet—from practically anywhere except Ponder's End and Peebles—who are on the track of the jewel stolen from the temple.

(*b*) Men with a grudge which has lasted as fresh as ever for thirty years.

(*c*) Master Criminals.

With regard to (*a*), I should advise James to try almost anything else first. I rather fancy that sinister jewel trackers have about reached saturation point. Besides, what I might call the villain-supplying nationalities have grown so absurdly touchy these days. Make your murderer a Chinaman now, and within a week of your story's appearance letters are pouring into the publisher's office, signed Disgusted—Peking—and Mother of Five—Hankow—protesting against the unfair libel. Go elsewhere and you run up against Paterfamilias—Java—and Fair Play—Tibet. It is not worth it.

And yet the idea of falling back on (*b*) is not agreeable. The age in which we live is so practical, so matter-of-fact. We are no longer able to believe as readily as our fathers did in the man who cherishes a grudge for a quarter of a century. It was all very well in the old days, when there were fewer distractions, but what with golf and tennis and cross-word puzzles, and the flat-race season and the jumping season, and looking after the car and airing the dog and having to learn how to score at contract bridge, it seems simply incredible that a man should be able to keep his mind on some unpleasantness which happened in the early spring of 1904.

Which brings us to the last class—Master Criminals.

The psychology of the Master Criminal is a thing I have never been able to understand. I can follow the reasoning of the man who, wishing to put by something for a rainy day, poisons an uncle, shoots a couple of cousins and forges a will. That is business. It is based on sound commercial principles. But the Master Criminal is simply a ditherer. He does not need money. He has got the stuff. What with the Delancy emeralds and the Stuyvesant pearls and the Montresor Holbein and the bearer bonds he stole from the bank, he must have salted away well over a million. Then what on earth does he want to go on for? Why not retire? But do you think you could drive that into a Master Criminal's head? Not in a million years. I have just been reading the latest story about one of these poor half-wits. This one, in order to go on being a Master Criminal, was obliged to live in a broken-down cellar on a smelly wharf on the river, posing as a lodging-house keeper. All he did with his time was chop wood in the back yard. And at a conservative estimate after paying salaries to his staff of one-eyed Chinamen, pock-marked Mexicans and knife-throwing deaf mutes, he must have been worth between two and three million pounds.

He could have had a yacht, a fleet of motor cars, a house in Grosvenor Square, a nice place in the country, a bit of shooting in Scotland, a few miles of fishing on some good river, a villa on the Riviera, and a racing stable. He could have run a paper, revived British opera and put on Shakespeare at popular prices. But no; he preferred to go on living in his riverside cellar, which was flooded every time there was a high tide, simply because he wanted to be a Master Criminal. One scarcely knows whether to laugh or weep.

THE ONE SATISFACTORY VILLAIN

I REMEMBER one Master Criminal, just as rich as this man, who set his whole organization at work for weeks digging a tunnel into a bank. And what do you think he got out of it? Twelve thousand pounds. Not guineas—pounds.

Twelve thousand pounds! Can you beat it! Just about what I am paid for this article.

Perhaps, on the whole, then, James, you had better avoid all three types of villain which I have mentioned and stick to the Fiend in Human Shape. This variety has the enormous advantage that he has not got to be made plausible. He is a homicidal lunatic, and, as such, can get away with anything. To the man with the thirty-year-old grudge we say, "But, my dear fellow, consider. If you stick that knife into Sir George, what of the future? What will you do in the long winter evenings with no dream of vengeance to nurse?" To the Master Criminal we point out that he is giving himself a lot of trouble to add to an income which is already absurdly large. He cannot like having to put on false whiskers and stand outside the hero's bedroom on a chilly night, pumping poison gas through it, or enjoy climbing up a slippery roof to drop cobras down the chimney. But the Fiend in Human Shape we merely pat encouragingly on the back and speed on his way with a cheery "Good luck, Fiend, old man! Go as far as you like!"

And he gnashes his teeth amiably and snaps into it with an animal snarl.

The Pocket Mystery Reader. Ed. by Lee Wright. NY: Pocket Books, 1942.

ACKNOWLEDGMENTS AND SOURCES